HIDDEN FIGURES
YOUNG READERS' EDITION

HIDDEN FIGURES

YOUNG READERS' EDITION

The untold **TRUE STORY**
of four African-American women
who helped launch our nation
into **SPACE**

MARGOT LEE SHETTERLY

THORNDIKE PRESS
A part of Gale, a Cengage Company

Farmington Hills, Mich • San Francisco • New York • Waterville, Maine
Meriden, Conn • Mason, Ohio • Chicago

Recommended for Middle Readers.
Copyright © 2016 by Margot Lee Shetterly.
Motion Picture artwork © Twentieth Century Fox Film Corporation.
Thorndike Press, a part of Gale, a Cengage Company.

**LIBRARY OF CONGRESS CIP DATA ON FILE.
CATALOGUING IN PUBLICATION FOR THIS BOOK
IS AVAILABLE FROM THE LIBRARY OF CONGRESS**

ISBN-13: 978-1-4328-4327-4 (hardcover)
ISBN-10: 1-4328-4327-3 (hardcover)

ISBN 13: 978-1-4328-5025-8 (pbk.)

Published in 2018 by arrangement with HarperCollins Children's Books,
an imprint of HarperCollins Publishers

Printed in the USA
2 3 4 5 6   28 27 26 25 24

*To my parents, Margaret G. Lee
and Robert B. Lee III,
and to all of the women at the NACA
and NASA who offered their shoulders
to stand on*

TABLE OF CONTENTS

PROLOGUE

Growing up in Hampton, Virginia, I assumed the face of science was brown like mine. My dad worked at the Langley Research Center at NASA, the National Aeronautics and Space Administration. He started there as an engineering intern in 1964 and retired as an internationally respected climate scientist in 2004. Our next-door neighbor taught physics. Our church pews were crowded with mathematicians. I knew so many African Americans working in science, math, and engineering that I thought that's just what black folks did.

My father, who as a high school student had wanted to study electrical engineering, lived a different story. "Become a physical education teacher," my grandfather told him. He thought my dad would have trouble finding work as an engineer. In the 1960s, most college-educated African Americans took teaching jobs or worked for the post office. As late as 1970, just 1 percent of all American engineers were black, and my father was one of them.

Because of my father's job, I was part of the NASA family. I grew up saving my allowance to buy tickets to ride ponies at the annual NASA carnival and sharing my Christmas wish list with the Santa at the NASA holiday party. On Thursday nights, I sat with my family and cheered for the Stars, my dad's NBA team (that's the NASA Basketball Association).

My Sunday school teacher worked at NASA as a "computer," doing the complex math for the aerospace engineers. She wasn't alone: from the 1940s through the 1970s, hundreds of women, many of whom were black, worked as mathematicians at NASA. It wasn't until I was older that I appreciated just how extraordinary this occupation was for black women in the South during the days of segregation. The first five women were hired at Langley as computers in 1935, and they were white. Ten years later, there were more than four hundred women working as mathematicians, and many of them were black.

The contributions made by these African-American women have never been heralded, but they deserve to be remembered — and not as a side note in someone else's account, but as the center of their own story. These women should be celebrated not just because they are black or because they are women, but because they are an important part of American history.

This is their story.

SETTING THE SCENE

Dorothy Vaughan, Mary Jackson, Katherine Johnson, and Christine Darden loved math. As children, they showed special skill in arithmetic, and they went on to study mathematics in college. After graduation they worked as teachers before going to work as "computers," or mathematicians, for the government's air and space program.

Over the years, hundreds of women worked as mathematicians for the federal agency called the NACA — the National Advisory Committee for Aeronautics — which researched and promoted the study of flight. But these women were among many who distinguished themselves with their talents and hard work.

Dorothy Vaughan was a pioneer. She joined the NACA in 1943, the first year the agency began hiring African-American women as computers, and she was the first to be promoted into a management position. She was a role model for other women, and she helped to steer the careers of many talented women who were joining the NACA.

Mary Jackson was the first African-American woman to move up the ranks and become an engineer at the NACA. She was a fighter, standing up for herself and for other women who deserved the chance to prove themselves. Her work helped to make supersonic aircraft fly higher and faster.

Katherine Johnson was an African-American woman who became an essential member of the team that put the first American in orbit around Earth. She was a dreamer and an independent thinker who was unafraid to imagine what others considered to be impossible. She helped do the math that was required to send the first men into space — and to bring them home safely.

Christine Darden was an African-American woman who became one of the world's leading experts on supersonic flight. She became the face of the next generation of female space scientists. Her groundbreaking research on predicting sonic booms is still used today.

The accomplishments of these four women were remarkable. But their work was even more impressive because it was achieved while living and working in the South during a time when racial discrimination was commonplace, and when most women with an interest in math were expected to become math teachers.

A Different Time

In the 1800s, after the Civil War, the government passed laws that ended slavery and granted full citizenship and voting rights to African Americans. Later, however, many state and local governments passed other laws that legalized racial segregation. These regulations, which were most common in the South, kept black people and white people apart in many situations.

They could not eat in the same restaurants.

They could not drink from the same water fountains.

They could not use the same restrooms.

They could not attend the same schools.

They could not ride in the same parts of buses.

They could not live in the same neighborhoods.

They could not receive care in the same

hospitals.

They could not visit the same beaches.

They could not compete on the same sports teams.

They could not sit in the same sections in movie theaters.

They could not marry someone of a different race.

They could not even be buried in the same cemeteries.

Technically, African Americans had the right to vote. However, many local laws made it impossible for them to do so. Some communities levied, or charged, poll taxes, or enforced literacy requirements or imposed other restrictions that made it difficult or impossible for black people to register and vote. And since people who were not registered to vote weren't allowed to serve on juries or run for political office, many African Americans were deprived of these civil rights as well.

During the 1930s, the United States experienced the Great Depression, a decade-long period of economic struggle. Jobs became difficult to find and wages decreased dramatically. All Americans suffered, but African Americans faced the most serious challenges in finding work.

For many African Americans, World War

II was an opportunity to make a better life for themselves and their families. Black men enlisted in the military in large numbers. Even though they served in separate black infantry regiments, usually overseen by white officers, they believed that their loyalty and patriotism would help blacks to earn rights that white citizens had. Women also enlisted in the army, where they were called WACs (for Women's Army Corps), and they served in all-female units in the navy, too. And for women like Dorothy Vaughan, Mary Jackson, Katherine Johnson, and Christine Darden, World War II opened the door to a career as a professional mathematician. Each of them found their way to the Langley Laboratory, where they met one another, and women like them: smart, brave, confident, and good at math. The war was changing the world, and it would change their lives as well.

A Door Opens

The newspaper ad caught the attention of many women. It read: "Reduce your household duties! Women who are not afraid to roll up their sleeves and do jobs previously filled by men should call the Langley Memorial Aeronautical Laboratory."

A few years earlier, an ad like this would have been unthinkable — most employers never would have considered a woman for a job that had always been performed by a man. But in the spring of 1943, with World War II in full swing and many men off serving in the military, the country needed all the help it could get. Employers were beginning to hire women to do jobs that had once belonged *only* to men.

This particular ad was placed by the National Advisory Committee for Aeronautics (NACA), a government agency dedicated to studying the science of flying. The NACA shared a campus with the US Army Air Corps in Hampton, Virginia, a city in the southeastern part of the state, next to the Chesapeake Bay.

The NACA's mission was important and unique: to help the United States develop the most powerful and efficient airplanes in the world. Airplanes moved military troops, tracked enemies, and launched bombs. World leaders felt that the country that ruled the skies would win the war. President Franklin D. Roosevelt believed in the importance of air power, so two years earlier, in 1941, he had challenged the nation to increase its production of airplanes to fifty thousand units a year. At that time, the industry had manufactured only three thousand planes a year.

The NACA and private industry were up for the challenge. By 1943, the American aircraft industry was the largest, most productive, and most sophisticated in the world, making three times more planes than the Germans, who were fighting on the other side of the war.

"Victory through Air Power!"

Before manufacturers built the airplanes, the designs were developed, tested, and refined at the Langley Memorial Aeronautical Laboratory, which was where the NACA had first begun its operations, in 1917. The engineers created wind tunnels to simulate, or imitate, different conditions a plane could encounter when flying. This helped the engineers to test airplane parts as well as whole aircraft, examining them for any problems, like air disturbance and uneven wing geometry.

After that testing, pilots flew the planes, trying to assess how the machines handled in the air. Did the aircraft roll unexpectedly? Did it stall? Was it hard to guide or maneuver? Making small changes to the design added up to a difference in performance. Even tiny improvements in speed and efficiency multiplied over millions of pilot miles added to a difference that could tip the balance of the war.

People working at Langley knew that they were doing their part to win the war. "Victory through air power!" said Henry Reid, the engineer-in-charge of the Langley Laboratory. And the workers took their mission to heart.

WANTED: Female Mathematicians

Each of the engineers at the Langley Memorial Aeronautical Laboratory required the support of a number of other workers: craftsmen to build the airplane models, mechanics to maintain the test tunnels, and "number crunchers" to process the data that was collected during the tests. For the engineers, a plane was basically a complex physics experiment. Physics is the science of matter, energy, and motion. Physics meant math, and math meant mathematicians. At the Langley Laboratory, mathematicians meant women.

Female mathematicians had been on the job at Langley since 1935. And it didn't take long for the women to show that they were just as good or even better at computing than many of the male engineers. But few of the women were granted the title "mathematician," which would have put them on equal footing with some male employees. Instead, they were classified as "subprofessionals," a title that meant they could be paid less.

At Langley, the female mathematicians were called "computers." They did the computations to turn the results of the raw data gathered by the engineers into a more useful form. Today we think of computers

A woman computer at Langley Memorial Aeronautical Laboratory with a calculating machine on her desk. NASA-Langley.

as machines, but in the 1940s, a computer was just someone whose job it was to do computations, a flesh-and-blood woman who was very good with numbers.

In 1943, it was difficult for the Langley Laboratory to find as many qualified women as they needed. A recruiter from the National Advisory Committee for Aeronautics visited colleges in search of young women with analytical or mathematical skills.

The Human Computers

When the managers couldn't satisfy the demand with only white employees, the government decided to hire African Americans. A civil rights leader named A. Philip Randolph encouraged President Roosevelt to sign an executive order — a law that ordered the desegregation of the federal government and defense industry and created the Fair Employment Practices Committee. This executive order opened up new and exciting opportunities for African Americans, allowing them to work side by side with white people during the war.

The federal government also helped create special training classes at black colleges, where people could learn the skills they would need to be successful in the war jobs. Black newspapers like the *Norfolk Journal and Guide* published articles telling their readers to apply for these new job openings. And there were many applicants! The applications were not supposed to consider race — a recent law had done away with the requirement that the application must include a photo — but it wasn't hard for employers to figure out which job candidates were black. African Americans did not have access to white colleges and universities, so black applicants came from black colleges, such as West Virginia State University, Howard University, Hampton Institute, and Arkansas Agricultural, Mechanical & Normal College. Many of the African-American candidates had years of teaching experience as well as math and science degrees.

Once hired, the black mathematicians were assigned to a separate work space in the Warehouse Building on the west side of the Langley campus. The East Area Computers were all white; the West Area Computers were all black, except for the supervisor and her assistant, who were white women.

There had always been African-American employees at Langley, but they had worked as janitors, cafeteria workers, mechanic's assistants, and groundskeepers. Hiring black mathematicians — that was something new. For the most part, the engineers welcomed extra hands, even if those hands were black. The Langley Laboratory was operating around the clock to test airplanes to be flown by American soldiers in the war: everyone had a job to do.

Hampton, Virginia, where the Langley campus was located, was very much a southern town. State law and Virginia custom meant that African Americans did

24

not ride the same buses or eat in the same cafeterias or use the same bathrooms as whites. The Langley staff had to prepare for the arrival of the African-American mathematicians. One of the tasks: creating metal bathroom signs that read "Colored Girls."

For the black women, the experience of working at a laboratory offered the chance to do interesting work that would help support the war effort. Walking into an unfamiliar environment wasn't easy for the women of the new West Area Computing Office, but each of them was eager for the opportunity to help their country and prove that they, too, could be excellent mathematicians.

The employees of the Langley Memorial Aeronautical Laboratory assemble for a visit from the secretary of the navy in 1943. NASA-Langley.

3

MOBILIZATION

There was no escaping the heat during the summer of 1943, especially for the African-American women working in Camp Pickett's laundry boiler plant. Camp Pickett was an army training center in central Virginia that processed eighteen thousand bundles of laundry each week. Inside the facility, the heat and humidity were so intense that the workers stepped outdoors into the 100-plus-degree summer heat to get relief.

The job at the plant was hard work. Some of the women loaded the soldiers' dirty laundry into the boilers. Others heaved the sopping clothes into the dryers. Another team worked the pressing machines, like cooks at a giant griddle. The laundry workers existed at the bottom of the war's great pyramid of employees. They earned forty

This laundry at the US Naval Air Station in Jacksonville, Florida, resembles the facility at Camp Pickett in Blackstone, Virginia. *US Navy Bureau of Naval Personnel Information Bulletin, June 1944.*

cents an hour — among the lowest wages of all war workers — but for women with few employment options, even that modest sum felt like a windfall.

Dorothy Vaughan considered applying for a job at the laundry. The thirty-two-year-old taught math at the black high school in Farmville, Virginia, about thirty miles from Camp Pickett. Her family was better off financially than many others — her husband's parents owned a barbershop, a pool hall, and a service station in town — but Dorothy wanted to find a job to earn extra money. While teaching offered status, it didn't pay well. Virginia's white public school teachers earned some of the lowest salaries in the United States, and black teachers in Virginia earned 50 percent less than that. Dorothy could earn twice her teacher's salary by working at the laundry.

Some women with Dorothy's education might have seen taking the laundry job as an unthinkable choice. Wasn't the purpose of a college degree to get away from dirty and difficult work? In addition, the camp was far enough away from Farmville that Dorothy would have to live in employee housing during the week and only go home on weekends.

But Dorothy didn't care. She would do whatever was necessary to save enough money so that her four children might be able to get the best education possible. She knew that schooling was the best way to prepare her children to live in a world that would require more of them than white children, and attempt to give them less in return.

Dorothy Vaughan's Childhood

Dorothy Vaughan was born in Kansas City, Missouri, in 1910. Her mother died when Dorothy was two years old, and her father remarried a few years later. Dorothy's stepmother encouraged her to succeed, teaching her how to read before she was old enough to start school. The family moved to West Virginia when Dorothy was eight.

Dorothy studied hard and became valedictorian of her high school class. She earned a full scholarship to Wilberforce University, the country's oldest private black college, located near Xenia, Ohio. The African Methodist Episcopal Sunday School Convention of West Virginia sponsored the scholarship.

At Wilberforce, Dorothy majored in math. She earned good grades, and one of her professors recommended her for graduate study in mathematics at Howard University, in Washington, DC. At the time, with the Depression still affecting the country, Dorothy's parents struggled to make enough money to support the family. Dorothy decided to turn down graduate school in order to take a job; the money she earned would contribute to her family's household and improve the chances that her younger sister might be able to follow her path to college. Dorothy looked for work as a teacher, the most stable career at the time for black women with a college degree.

After graduation in 1929, Dorothy taught math and English at a black school in rural Tamms, Illinois, a region that depended on cotton farming. That year the Depression caused a collapse in cotton prices that hit the area so hard that the local school board closed Dorothy's school, leaving no public education available for African-American students. Dorothy was forced to look for work again, and she found another teaching job at a school in coastal North Carolina. But things weren't any better there. That school also ran out of money in the middle of the year. Dorothy returned home and worked as a waitress at a hotel until 1931, when she took a job teaching in Farmville, Virginia.

It was in Farmville that Dorothy met Howard Vaughan, a tall, charismatic bachelor who worked as a bellman at various luxury hotels. Howard traveled south to hotels in Florida in the winter and north to hotels in upstate New York and Vermont in the summer. In between jobs, he always returned to Farmville, where his family lived.

Dorothy and Howard fell in love, married,

31

and settled in Farmville. She attended Beulah African Methodist Episcopal Church with her family and played piano on Sunday mornings. She had found steady work and a fulfilling life in the small town. But then World War II started, bringing with it more job opportunities and the hope for even better times ahead.

War Work

In the early 1940s, the United States government spread the word far and wide that it was hiring. Bulletins listing civil service jobs — nonmilitary government jobs — plastered the walls at local post offices. And it was on a trip to the Farmville post office during the spring of 1943 that Dorothy saw a notice for the laundry job at Camp Pickett. But as she glanced over the other bulletins, the word "mathematics" caught her eye. She looked more closely and learned that a federal agency in Hampton, Virginia, was looking for women to fill a number of mathematical jobs at a facility specializing in the development of airplanes.

Dorothy assumed the bulletin was meant for the eyes of the white, well-to-do students at the all-female State Teachers College in Farmville. It never occurred to her that the Langley Memorial Aeronautical Laboratory would accept an application from an African-American woman.

But during World War II, the United States asked for help from all of its citizens. Workers — black, white, and from every other ethnic background, women as well as men — were needed, and black newspapers spread the word about war jobs.

In the first week of May 1943, the *Norfolk Journal and Guide* published an article that caught Dorothy's eye. "Paving the Way for Women Engineers," read the headline. The accompanying photo showed eleven well-dressed African-American women in front of Hampton Institute's Bemis Laboratory, graduates of Engineering for Women, a war training class. Maybe there *were* opportunities for African-American women who loved numbers. Dorothy decided to fill out an application.

Jobs, Good Jobs, and *Very* Good Jobs
In Dorothy Vaughan's world, there were black jobs, and there were *good* black jobs. Sorting laundry, making beds in white people's houses, working in tobacco plants — those were black jobs.

Owning a barbershop or a small business, working in the post office or on the railroad — those were good black jobs.

Being a teacher or a preacher, a doctor or a lawyer — those were *very* good black jobs.

But the job at the aeronautical laboratory was something entirely new, something so unusual it hadn't been dreamed of yet. It was an opportunity that had the potential to change the future of Dorothy's family. Even if the war ended in six months or a year, earning a much higher salary for that brief time could help her save money for her children's education.

That spring, Dorothy Vaughan filled out and mailed two job applications, one to work at the Camp Pickett laundry and one to work as a mathematician at Langley. The application for the laundry job was straight-forward. There was such demand for laundry workers that she couldn't imagine not being hired.

The other application asked for Dorothy's work history, references, schools attended, languages spoken. One question asked: "How soon could you be ready to start work?"

She filled in the blank: *48 hours.*

If she got the job, she could be ready to go in forty-eight hours. Because a chance like that might never come around again.

A New Beginning

In the fall of 1943, Dorothy Vaughan started the school year teaching math at R. R. Moton, the black high school in Farmville, Virginia, just as she had for the past twelve years. She loved being a teacher, and she dedicated herself to helping her students as much as she could while waiting for a response to the job applications she had submitted a few months earlier.

Dorothy had plenty to keep her busy. The high school had been built for 180 students, but more than 300 now squeezed into the classrooms. She taught algebra in the school's overcrowded auditorium with two other classes taking place in the same space. After school, she tutored students who needed more help and spent time working with the school's parent-teacher association.

Outside of school, Dorothy was a founding board member of the Farmville chapter of the NAACP, the National Association for the Advancement of Colored People, a civil rights group.

"What Can We Do to Win the War?"

World War II was never far from anyone's mind. That fall, the high school's 4-H club made care packages for departing servicemen and hosted a community discussion titled "What Can We Do to Win the War?" The school sold war stamps to raise money for the military. The community held going-away parties and feasts for the young men heading off to the front lines of combat.

Dorothy updated her classes and added a unit called Wartime Mathematics, where she taught students how to use math to follow a household budget and manage wartime ration books, coupon books that allowed each family only a limited amount of various supplies such as flour and sugar.

Then, in November, a letter from the National Advisory Committee for Aeronautics finally arrived. "You are hereby appointed Mathematician, Grade P-1, with pay at the rate of $2,000 per annum," the letter said. That was more than twice the $850 annual salary she earned as a teacher.

When Dorothy thought about the civil service jobs she had applied for, she had mixed feelings. She was a wife and a mother of four children. The job at the Langley Laboratory was a full-time position, six days a week. If she accepted the job, she would have to move four hours away from her children, and she'd only be able to come back home to see them on holidays.

But Dorothy knew this was a very good job, one that would allow her to help her family. So she accepted. She shared the news with her family and friends. Her students were sad to see their teacher Mrs. Vaughan leave the school. The townspeople found out about Dorothy's decision when they read a notice in the Farmville section of the *Norfolk Journal and Guide.* It read: "Mrs. D. J. Vaughan, instructor in mathematics at the high school for several years, has accepted a position at Langley Field, Va."

Dorothy didn't like long good-byes. "I'll be back for Christmas," she told her four young children. She was sad to leave them, but she knew that her children would be well cared for at home in Farmville. They lived in a rambling Victorian house with their grandparents, and they were surrounded by dozens of aunts and uncles and cousins. Dorothy's children would miss their mother, but their daily schedules wouldn't change much.

For twelve years Dorothy had walked out of her front door and turned left to walk to the school where she worked. But on the morning she left for her new job at the Langley Memorial Aeronautical Laboratory, she turned in the opposite direction. And she didn't look back.

Leaving Home

Dorothy Vaughan rode a Greyhound bus 137 miles from Farmville to Newport News, Virginia. While on the bus she had plenty of time to think. What would it be like to work with white people? Would she sit side by side with young women like the ones at the State Teachers College? How would she endure the time away from her children and family?

Mile after mile, Dorothy watched the gentle hills rising and falling outside her window. She refused to feel any self-doubt. Her country needed her, and she was ready and eager to do her part to support the war effort and her family.

5

THE DOUBLE V

In the early 1940s, the Hampton Roads area was bustling with newcomers. The cities around the harbor — Newport News and Hampton to the north, and Portsmouth, Norfolk, and Virginia Beach to the south — had welcomed hundreds of thousands of new residents since the start of World War II. Between 1940 and 1942, the region's population had increased by more than 50 percent.

The area had emerged as a powerful military capital, and most of the jobs there were now related to the war. Much of the work belonged to women. The sight of women wearing coveralls and working at filling stations, a job that used to be just for men, no longer turned heads. Women now did all kinds of jobs — shined shoes, worked in the shipyard, and staffed offices. With men off to fight on the front lines, woman-power picked up the slack.

The war operated around the clock — three eight-hour shifts — and many businesses tried to keep pace. Some stores stayed open long hours. The movie theater showed movies from 11:00 a.m. to midnight, often featuring films with a strong dose of patriotism. Banks stayed open late to cash checks for workers.

All of the new residents needed places to live. Landlords doubled their rents and still had long waiting lists. Water systems, electrical plants, schools, and hospitals struggled to keep up with the growing population. The government addressed the shortage by building 5,200 new houses in the East End of Newport News. Of those, 1,200 homes were built for African Americans in a separate subdivision known as Newsome Park.

Welcome
Dorothy Vaughan arrived in Newport News on a Thursday and started work at the Langley Memorial Aeronautical Laboratory the following Monday. The personnel department kept a file of available houses for new employees, divided by race to comply with the custom of segregation. Five dollars

40

a week got Dorothy a room of her own and two meals a day in the home of a black couple in their sixties who were willing to take in a boarder. The house was located in the East End, not far from the newly built housing development Newsome Park. The houses in the city's East End neighborhood were well maintained, surrounded by thriving local businesses, and occupied by members of a growing middle class.

City buses and trolleys circulated through the neighborhood from morning until night, as employees punched out from one shift and met workers coming in for the next shift. The buses always seemed crowded, and the race-specific laws made commuting more difficult. Whites had to enter and exit from the front of the bus, while blacks had to go in and out of the back, behind what was known as the Colored Line. Those in the back of the bus had to stand if the white section was full. When the buses were short on conductors, blacks had to enter at the front and push their way to the back section, then do the same in reverse to get off the bus. Blacks caught in the white section were fined or arrested. Even whites complained about the jostling and scrambling caused by the rules.

A sign from the Newport News, Virginia, bus station in 1954. **Citizen's Rapid Transit Company. Virginia?: s.n., 19—.** **Broadside Collection, Library of Virginia.**

Race and Patriotism

In Hampton Roads and across the country, relationships between blacks and whites became strained. Overcrowded buses; six-day workweeks; constant noise and construction; shortages of sugar, coffee, butter, and meat — all of these factors came together to create tension.

This was not a new problem. Two years earlier, in his 1941 State of the Union address, President Franklin D. Roosevelt had promised that "men of every creed and every race, wherever they lived in the world" were entitled to "Four Freedoms" — freedom of speech, freedom of worship, freedom from want, and freedom from fear. He pledged that the United States would help to overcome dictators in other countries who would deny other people their freedoms.

African Americans were sympathetic to the needs of oppressed people around the world. They shared in the horror when they learned about the acts of the Germans against their Jewish citizens — limiting the jobs they could have, imprisoning them, denying them citizenship, treating them with violence, segregating them into ghettos, working them to death in slave camps, and having them killed. How could black Americans learn about the way the Jews were treated without comparing some of these experiences to some of their own struggles against slavery, unfair treatment, and violence at home?

For generations, African Americans had been promised an end to discrimination. But instead of greater freedom, the period between World War I and World War II — 1918 to 1941 — saw segregation harden and become the law of the land. As America made the decision to join the fighting in World War II, African Americans pressured the government to open the war jobs to their community. Leaders like A. Philip Randolph, who had helped make the Fair Employment Practices laws a reality, asked the country to show its patriotism by treating all of its citizens fairly.

Black newspapers spoke out on the issue. "Help us to get some of the blessings of democracy here at home first before you jump on the 'free other peoples' bandwagon and tell us to go forth and die in a foreign land," said P. B. Young, the owner of the *Norfolk Journal and Guide,* in a 1942 editorial. Should African Americans fight for freedom overseas when they did not experience it for themselves at home?

James Thompson, a twenty-six-year-old cafeteria worker, made his case in a letter to the *Pittsburgh Courier:* "Being an American of dark complexion, these questions flash through my mind: . . . 'Is the kind of America I know worth defending?' . . . 'Will colored Americans suffer still the indignities that have been heaped upon them in the past?' These and other questions need answering: I want to know, and I believe every colored American, who is thinking, wants to know."

What are we fighting for? This was the question asked by many African Americans in private and in public. African Americans were loyal to their country. They had a deep and abiding belief in the possibility of democracy. When Pearl Harbor was attacked and the United States joined the fighting in World War II, the African-American community closed ranks, as they had done in previous times of war. They geared up to fight for their country's future and for their own.

From this divide, between feeling black and feeling American, came the idea of the double victory. James Thompson expressed the idea in his letter to the *Pittsburgh Courier:* "Let colored Americans adopt the double VV for double victory; the first V for victory over our enemies from without, the second V for victory over our enemies within. For surely those who perpetrate these ugly prejudices here are seeking to destroy our democratic form of government just as surely as the Axis forces."

Dorothy Vaughan understood the importance of the Double V — victory in the war and victory in the civil rights struggle at home. By accepting her post as a mathematician, she believed she was working toward both goals.

On December 1, 1943, the leaders of the United States, Great Britain, and Russia concluded a conference during which they planned a summer invasion of France. It was an invasion that would become a turning point in the war and that eventually became known as D-day.

On the same day, Dorothy Vaughan stepped behind the Colored Line on the bus and headed to her first day of work at the Langley Memorial Aeronautical Laboratory.

6

THE "COLORED" COMPUTERS

On her first day of work at Langley, Dorothy Vaughan spent the morning in the personnel department filling out paperwork. As part of her orientation, she held up her right hand and swore the United States civil service oath of office: "I, Dorothy Vaughan, do solemnly swear that I will support and defend the Constitution of the United States against all enemies, foreign and domestic. . . ."

She took the pledge seriously, but it was her identification badge that made her feel like an official employee. The badge — a blue metal circle featuring an image of her face with the winged NACA logo on either side — granted her access to the various facilities at the Langley Laboratory.

Since its establishment in 1917, the Langley Memorial Aeronautical Laboratory's operations had been concentrated on the campus of Langley Field, an Army Air Corps base located on the eastern bank of Hampton's Back River. The Service Building, where Dorothy went through orientation, was one of the oldest buildings on the field. Year after year, the number of buildings had grown, until the laboratory decided to expand to the area on the western side of the river. That land was still a forest when the construction began, and employees joked about having to work in such a remote place. The weekly Langley employee newsletter *Air Scoop* described it as a "land of desolation, a land of marshes and mosquitoes."

After Dorothy finished the morning's paperwork, she boarded a campus shuttle bus that drove her to the end of a forested back road connecting the East Side of the Langley campus with the West Side. She looked around at the strange landscape of two-story brick offices and construction sites with half-finished buildings. Towering behind one of the buildings was a gigantic three-story-high ribbed-metal pipe. It was part of a wind tunnel called the Sixteen-Foot High-Speed Tunnel, which was used for experiments on airplanes. To make the

The West Side of Langley campus in 1941, with the East Side in the background. At the left is the Sixteen-Foot High-Speed Tunnel. This is before they camouflaged the buildings. NASA-Langley

scene even more unusual, all of the buildings had been painted dark green to camouflage them against possible attacks from America's wartime enemies.

The shuttle bus stopped to let Dorothy off at the front door of an office building called the Warehouse Building. She went inside and found rooms filled with desks arranged classroom style. There were office-bright ceiling lights and narrow windows that looked out over the construction going on outside. From inside the rooms, Dorothy heard a new, unfamiliar sound: the steady beat of mechanical calculating machines, so big they each took up an entire desktop. It was like listening to a parade of drums: each time a click when a number was entered, a drumbeat when the operations key was hit, and a full drumroll when the machine ran through a complex calculation.

The same scene and the same sounds played in all the rooms where the women were working. Women were performing the same work at a similar place on the East Side. The only difference between the East Computers and the West Computers was obvious: all of the women sitting at the desks in Dorothy's work space were black.

Take a Seat

The room for the West Area computing pool was set up for about twenty workers. As members of a pool, each woman had to be ready to work on any mathematical assignment that came through the door. Because the engineering problems that the Langley Laboratory worked on were so complex, the problems had to be broken down into smaller parts, with each part assigned to a different woman.

Dorothy Vaughan took a seat, and the

women welcomed her. Most had graduated from black colleges like Hampton Institute, the Virginia State College for Negroes, or Arkansas Agricultural, Mechanical & Normal College. Many of the women had years of teaching experience; others were starting their first jobs, just out of college.

Quite a few of the women belonged to the same civic organizations, churches, and Greek letter organizations, such as Alpha Kappa Alpha or Delta Sigma Theta. Dorothy realized that by working in Langley's West Computing section, she was in one of the world's most exclusive groups. In 1940, just 2 percent of all black women earned college degrees, and 60 percent of those women became teachers, most in public elementary and high schools. At a time when just 10 percent of white women and not even a third of white men had earned college degrees, the West Computers had found jobs at the "single best and biggest aeronautical research complex in the world."

At the front of the room, like teachers in a classroom, sat two white women, the West Computing section head and her assistant. The work that came to a particular section usually flowed from the top of the pyramid down: engineers came to the head of the entire computing operation, who handed down tasks to each section head, who then divided up the work among the women in her section. Over time, some of the engineers developed favorites and brought assignments directly to the section head or even to a particular human computer.

Dorothy was a welcome addition to the computer pool. The women had too much work to do in too little time. The National Advisory Committee for Aeronautics planned to double the size of Langley's West Area in the next three years. When Dorothy arrived, the agency was scrambling to keep up with the American aircraft industry, which had gone from the *country's* forty-third largest industry in 1938 to the *world's* number one by 1943.

Trouble in the Lunchroom

In the middle of the day, the women of West Computing walked as a group over to the cafeteria. Langley was so crowded that each team had a designated thirty-minute window for lunch, just enough time for a quick meal and a little conversation.

Most groups sat together out of habit. For Dorothy and the West Computers, segregated seating was required. The women of West Computing were the only black women professionals at the laboratory, not exactly excluded but not quite included, either. A white cardboard sign on a table in the back of the cafeteria said "Colored Computers" in crisply stenciled black letters. It was the only sign in the cafeteria; no other group needed assigned seating.

This kind of racial insult was all too common. It was the kind of subtle jab that African Americans had learned to tolerate, if not accept, in order to function in their daily lives. The women probably expected it, but in the environment of the laboratory, a place that had chosen them for their intellectual talents, the sign seemed particularly offensive.

At first the women tried to ignore the sign. They pushed it aside and tried to pretend it wasn't there. In the office, the women felt equal, but in the cafeteria and the bathrooms, the "Colored" signs were a reminder that some were more equal than others.

A mathematician named Miriam Mann finally decided she didn't want to look at that cafeteria sign anymore. Not even five feet tall, her feet just grazing the floor when she sat down, Miriam had a huge personality. Dorothy and the other West Computers watched as Miriam slipped the sign into her purse. Her small act of defiance made them all feel a bit anxious but also empowered.

But the next day, the sign reappeared.

Miriam removed it again.

This happened again and again for weeks. Sometimes the sign disappeared for a few days or a week — sometimes longer — but each time it was eventually replaced with an identical twin.

As the sign drama played itself out in the Langley cafeteria, an important civil rights case was playing out in the courts. Irene Morgan, an employee at the Baltimore-based aircraft manufacturer Glenn L. Martin Company, worked on an airplane production line. In the summer of 1944, Morgan traveled on the Greyhound bus to her hometown in Gloucester County, Virginia, next door to Hampton. On the return trip she was arrested because she refused to move to the back of the bus. The NAACP Legal Defense Fund defended Morgan, and in 1946, the US Supreme Court ruled in *Morgan v. Virginia* that segregation on interstate buses was illegal.

What were the women at West Computing doing making such a fuss about a sign in the cafeteria? Outside Langley, serious civil rights battles were being fought on the streets and in the courts.

"They are going to fire you over that sign, Miriam," her husband said.

But being black in America was a never-ending series of decisions about when to fight and when to let things go. "Then they're just going to have to do it," Miriam said.

Numbers Are Color-Blind

Miriam and her husband lived near the Hampton Institute campus, not far from where Dorothy lived. Although the students were predominantly black, the school's president and many professors were white. Malcolm MacLean, the head of the school, was determined that the school be committed to participation in the war effort.

Under MacLean's direction, the college established a US naval training school, effectively turning the campus into an active military base. Military police manned the campus entrances and patrolled the grounds. More than a thousand black naval recruits from around the county were sent to the school to learn how to repair airplane and boat engines.

The school was also dedicated to providing engineering, science, and war management training programs for people who wanted to work for the government and help America fight the war. As part of the program, men and women, including many of the women now working in the West Area Computing office, crowded into Hampton Institute classrooms to learn everything from radio science to chemistry to engineering. At a war labor conference that Hampton Institute hosted in 1942, the college president told attendees that the war could be "the greatest break in history for minority groups."

Many local whites didn't approve of MacLean's progressive ideas. They were particularly upset about how comfortable he was with socializing with black people as well as white people. In speeches, MacLean urged administrators at white colleges to hire black professors. He entertained blacks and whites together in the president's residence. He even danced with a Hampton student at a school dance, causing a scandal. He believed in the Double V — victory in the war effort and victory on the home front — and wanted to help African Americans advance in American society.

On the Langley campus, most of the engineers were conflicted on the issue of race mixing. They may not have thought about inviting their black colleagues to their homes for dinner, but at the office they were friendly. The same attitude applied to women in the workforce. When there was so much work to be done, the engineers were open to giving a smart person — black or white, male or female — the chance to work hard and get the numbers right.

The Sisterhood

As far as the West Computers were concerned, they assumed that they would have to prove themselves equal to or better than the white mathematicians. Because of the discrimination, they believed that African Americans needed to be twice as good to get half as far as their white counterparts.

The West Computers rejected all notions of being inferior because they were black or female, and they banded together like sisters to help each other at work. They double-checked one another's work and policed each other to prevent tardiness, sloppy appearance, or the perception of bad behavior. They fought against negative stereotypes. They knew they stood for something bigger than themselves as individuals.

Miriam Mann and the other women were no doubt delighted that, at some point during the war, the "Colored Computers" sign disappeared from the cafeteria. The segregated office and separate bathrooms remained, but the Battle of the West Area Cafeteria was over. Even without the sign, the West Computers still sat together at the same table. Now, however, they were able to enjoy their lunch and each other's company without staring at a humiliating sign.

Many of the relationships that began in those early days in West Computing blossomed into lifetime friendships. Dorothy Vaughan, Miriam Mann, and the other women of West Computing became a sisterhood inside and outside of work. For ambitious young women with mathematical minds, there wasn't a better job in the world.

WAR BIRDS

African Americans carefully read every newspaper article about the Tuskegee Airmen, a group of black military pilots who fought during World War II. As with any other fliers, their lives depended on knowing their plane's strengths and weaknesses, and every response it would make as it waltzed through the sky. By the summer of 1944, the men of the 332nd Fighter Group were flying North American P-51 Mustangs.

"It's best described as a 'pilot's airplane,' " said an American military official in a front-page article in the *Washington Post*. "It's very fast and handles beautifully at high speeds." With a big four-blade propeller and a Rolls-Royce Merlin engine, the Mustang sped across the sky like a four-hundred-miles-per-hour racehorse. The Tuskegee Air-

The Tuskegee Airmen in 1942–1943, location unknown. US Air Force.

men and lots of other pilots considered it to be the best plane in the world.

"I will get you up in the air, let you do your job, and bring you back to earth safely," promised the Mustang to its pilots, like a trusted horse to its rider. And helping the plane to make good on that promise was now part of Dorothy Vaughan's full-time job.

The Secret Weapon
But Dorothy couldn't really talk to her friends and family about her work. During

World War II, the National Advisory Committee for Aeronautics wanted to defeat Germany by air, both by creating planes capable of destroying their targets and by coming up with technological advancements that would give the United States a military advantage. The Langley Laboratory was one of the United States' most powerful weapons, a secret weapon hidden in plain sight in a small southern Virginia town.

While the performance of the Mustang airplanes fighting overseas was a topic of front-page news, the daily work of the West Computers and the others in the lab was considered sensitive and even secret. Bosses told their employees to stay on the lookout for spies disguised as soldiers or people who might try to get valuable information from laboratory employees. *Air Scoop,* the newspaper of the NACA, sounded the alarm: "You tell it to someone who repeats it to someone . . . so SOMEONE you know . . . may die!"

The Langley employees took the warning to heart. Even if they had wanted to talk about their work, they would have found it difficult to find someone outside of the lab who would understand what they were talking about.

Off campus, people around town often

found the Langley employees a bit peculiar. They had strange accents from other parts of the country. Many of them wore rumpled shirts with no ties, and some wore sandals or sported beards. Locals called them "brain busters" or "NACA nuts"; the less polite called them "weirdos."

"What Makes Things Fly?"

The pace of discovery and invention was so fast at Langley that an entry-level position there was considered by many people to be like studying at the world's best engineering school. In addition to receiving on-the-job training, employees had the chance to take classes in math and physics and other subjects that would help them further understand how to design better planes.

And that's what Dorothy did. With the goal of turning women math teachers into crack junior engineers, the laboratory sponsored a crash course in engineering physics for the newly arrived computers. Two days a week after work, Dorothy Vaughan and the other new mathematicians filed into a makeshift classroom at the laboratory for an intensive class in the fundamental theory of aerodynamics, which is the study of objects moving through the air. They also attended a weekly two-hour laboratory session for hands-on training in one of the wind tunnels, and they had an average of four hours of homework on top of their six-day workweek.

What makes things fly? Dorothy asked herself all day long at her new job. She had never flown on a plane and had never before given much thought to the question. The first course she took at Langley taught her the basics of aerodynamics. She learned that when a wing moves through the air, the air gets cut into two parts. There is slower-moving airflow on the bottom of the wing, and faster-moving airflow on the top. This creates two different pressures, and it's this difference in pressure that creates lift, the almost magical force that causes the wing — and the plane attached to it — to rise into the sky.

It's important to keep air smoothly flowing around the plane. Turbulence or sudden gusts of wind can make a plane hard to control. One of the NACA's greatest achievements was designing wings that allowed planes to move easily through the air.

Today we take many of these design elements for granted, but each change came about after a series of experiments and mathematical computations — and luck. The first inventors made some assumptions, built a plane, tried to fly it, and if they didn't die in the process, they applied what they learned to the next attempt.

By the time Dorothy was on the job, the task of modifying airplane design had been turned over to the aeronautical engineers and the test pilots who flew the planes directly into their weak spots. Each time the pilots pushed the aircraft to the limit, they helped generate data that could be used to identify ways to make a good plane even better. The test pilots also risked their lives and the loss of a very expensive piece of equipment.

To make the job easier, researchers developed wind tunnels that allowed them to test model planes without the danger of flying a real plane. At its simplest, a wind tunnel was a big box attached to a powerful fan. The basic idea behind the wind tunnel was that air moving at a certain speed over a stationary object was similar to moving the object through the air at the same speed. Engineers blasted air over full-sized aircraft, scale models, or individual parts, such as wings or bodies. By closely observing how the air flowed around the object, the engineers could assess how the object would fly through the air. Langley built different wind tunnels to test specific features of the planes. There was even a tunnel called the Full-Scale Tunnel, which opened wide enough to swallow a full-sized plane.

Running the electricity-hungry wind tunnels wasn't always easy for the laboratory, because the local power company rationed electricity during the war, including for the laboratory. The NACA solved the problem by running some of their tests into the wee hours, and people living near Langley complained about the roar of the tunnels while they were trying to sleep. Despite the challenges, building wind tunnels that were quite similar to real-world conditions was one of the keys to the NACA's success.

Making a Good Plane Better

No organization came close to Langley in the quality and range of wind tunnel research data. It wasn't good enough to say a plane flew well or badly. Engineers tried to measure how a plane performed, so they developed a nine-page checklist. These experiments generated data — numbers, lots and lots of numbers. And the raw data from the tests then went to the desks of Dorothy Vaughan and the other female computers for analysis.

An airplane wasn't one machine for a single purpose. It was a complex machine that could be tweaked to perform different kinds of tasks. The airplane names or designations reflected their use: fighters — also called "pursuit planes" — were assigned the letter *F* or the letter *P*. The letter *C* identified cargo planes, which were built to transport military goods and troops. *B* was for bombers, and *X* marked the spot of experimental planes still in development. Planes lost their *X* designation once they went into production. For example, the B-29 was the final version of the XB-29.

Engineers worked hard to make each version of an aircraft better and more stable than the previous one. Discoveries large and small contributed to the speed, maneuverability, and safety of the machines. As World War II approached its peak in 1945, almost every American military airplane being produced in factories had features that were based on the research results and recommendations of the NACA.

Whether data came from the wind tunnels, test flights, or theoretical models, it eventually reached the women computers so they could use their sharp pencils and sharp minds to figure out what the numbers meant. Instead of looking at just a few numbers, they looked at extremely large sets of numbers, which could be used to find

The B-29 Superfortress was a four-engine propeller-driven heavy bomber used during World War II. It was the most expensive aircraft designed during the war. **US Air Force.**

patterns or trends in the ways the airplanes performed. What Dorothy and the other women at the laboratory worked on was usually a small portion of a larger task. The work was carved up into smaller pieces for quick, efficient, and accurate processing. By the time the work arrived on the computers' desks, it might be just a set of equations and numbers. Sometimes they didn't even know what kind of plane had been tested, or what the engineers were hoping to understand from their research. Once a woman finished a particular job, the calculations were taken to the engineers, who used them to improve airplane designs.

The computers' work was essential but largely uncelebrated. "Woe unto thee if they shall make thee a computer," joked a column in *Air Scoop.* "For the Project Engineer will take credit for whatsoever thou doth that is clever and full of glory. But if he slippeth up, and maketh a wrong calculation, . . . he shall lay the mistake at thy door when he is called to account and he shall say, 'What can you expect from girl computers anyway?' "

But sometimes a breakthrough was so important that everyone got credit. When the Boeing B-29 Superfortress was finished, it became a symbol of United States technological progress — and its ability to bring destruction to its enemies. "There is no one in the laboratory who should feel that he or she did not have a part in the bombing of Japan," the NACA director said to the lab employees. "The engineers who assisted, the mechanics and model-makers who did their share, the computers who worked up the data, the secretaries who typed and retyped the results, and the janitors and maids who kept the tunnel clean and suitable for work, all made their contribution to the final bombing of Japan."

Dorothy knew that her work was making a difference in the outcome of the war. She read the news accounts of how the B-29s — capable of flying farther, faster, and with a heavier bomb load than any plane in history — dropped precision bombs over Japan from high in the sky. Dorothy found her work more intense and interesting than she had imagined, and she knew she wanted to stay for the duration of the war — and maybe longer. There was no doubt about it, Dorothy Vaughan had become one of the "NACA nuts."

THE DURATION

Though Dorothy Vaughan loved her new job in Hampton, and was proud to be helping her country with the war effort, she missed her children terribly. She sometimes worked eighteen-hour days, and the demands of her job made it difficult for her to get home except for during holidays. And it seemed like the minute she walked through the door at the family house back in Farmville, it was time for her to turn around and head back to Newport News. When she could go home, the back-and-forth lifestyle was taking a toll. Dorothy wanted something more permanent.

Like most of the computers at the Langley Memorial Aeronautical Laboratory, Dorothy was a temporary war service employee. She didn't know when — or if — the laboratory would offer her a permanent job. Dorothy knew what she wanted her future to look like, so in July 1944 she signed a lease on a new two-bedroom apartment in Newsome Park. Dorothy wanted her children eventually to live with her for good in Newport News. This two-bedroom apartment would be a start.

But finding the right house hadn't been easy. There weren't enough homes available to meet the demands of the growing African-American population. Dorothy chose a neighborhood near where she had been living for the previous nine months. It included black families from all income levels; domestic workers lived next to doctors, lawyers next to laborers, small-business owners next to civil servant mathematicians. All were welcome. Dorothy's new home was identical to the 1,199 others that had been built in the same subdivision.

Newsome Park was also designed to keep morale high among the wartime workers who had to work long hours under stressful conditions. The Newsome Park residents loved that their neighborhood had a community center with a kitchen and banquet space, rooms for club meetings, and basketball and tennis courts. They even had a baseball diamond. And the shopping center included a grocery store, drugstore, barbershop, beauty parlor, cleaners, and a TV repair shop. A nursery school and a new elementary school were in walking distance from her new apartment.

Dorothy's mother-in-law tried to discourage the move. "You're not going to take my babies," she said to Dorothy. Dorothy appreciated her mother-in-law's help all the months she'd been away, but now she needed her children to be close to her.

A year after Dorothy left Farmville, her children moved into the apartment in Newsome Park. They started at Newsome Park Elementary School in the fall of 1944. Her husband continued to travel with his job as a bellman. He came down to visit when he could, but he didn't stay long.

Victory over Japan
By 1945, five out of ten people in southeastern Virginia worked for the government. Housing developments sprawled for miles. The community was built around the business of war. But people were starting to wonder what a defense industry boomtown would become during a time of peace.

The answer came on V-J Day, Victory over Japan Day. On August 14, 1945, at 7:00 p.m., newscasters announced that World

War II was over. All over town, soldiers and civilians streamed into the streets. Business owners locked their doors and joined the celebrations that went on through the night. People paraded down the streets and workers held hands to form human chains as they danced around cars. Makeshift confetti rained down from windows onto the streets below.

But after the initial celebrations and parties, uncertainty settled in. Three weeks after V-J Day, the *Norfolk Journal and Guide* reported layoffs of fifteen hundred Newport News shipyard workers and a "decrease for women workers, both white and colored." Returning servicemen were expected to have first claim on the jobs that remained in the peacetime economy.

With the return of the men who had been fighting overseas, the demand for women workers dropped. Two million American women — black and white alike — received "pink slips," or notices that they were losing their jobs, even before the war officially ended. Some women looked forward to going home. Others enjoyed their jobs and their paychecks, and they didn't want to go back to the traditional female roles in the kitchen and nursery.

"Many husbands will return home to find

that the helpless little wives they left behind have become grown, independent women," wrote a female columnist in the *Norfolk Journal and Guide.*

Postwar Prejudice

Almost immediately after V-J Day, some employers returned to their policies of not hiring African Americans. With the labor market changing, the dream that many black leaders had of establishing permanent economic opportunity began to slip away.

No one was more opposed to opening hiring policies to African Americans than Virginia's Democratic senator Harry Byrd, who called the policy "the most dangerous idea ever seriously considered." Byrd's family had built a newspaper and apple-growing fortune, and he treated segregation as a religion. He ran a political machine that kept the poor of all races divided against one another.

Dorothy, like so many of the others who had come to Hampton Roads during the war, didn't want to return to her former life. She assumed that she was going to keep her job and continue with her new life.

It wasn't a risk-free bet. Dorothy committed to the lease on the apartment in Newsome Park before Langley converted her

Harry F. Byrd was a white separatist who favored racial segregation. He served as governor of Virginia from 1926 to 1930 and as a senator from Virginia from 1933 to 1965.
United States Library of Congress.

wartime employee status to that of permanent civil service employee. She didn't want to wait to put down roots in her new home, even though it soon became apparent that losing the apartment was still a possibility. Dorothy and the others who lived in her neighborhood learned that some local officials wanted to demolish Newsome Park and redevelop the neighborhood. And federal authorities planned to pry the houses off their foundations and send them to "war-devastated populations in Europe."

The residents went back and forth with the government over the status of their neighborhood, which they had come to love. The government said that Newsome Park was "not temporary in character," yet "not permanent in its current location." Though they lived in a state of limbo, the people of Newsome Park were determined to do everything they could to keep their community alive.

Life in Newport News was an adjustment for Dorothy's children, who missed their small-town freedom and the space at the big house in Farmville. But as the months passed, the family settled in. Dorothy had become quite close to her fellow West Computer Miriam Mann. They were friends both at work and at home, and their families had become like one large extended family. When Dorothy and Miriam learned that the famous African-American singer Marian Anderson was going to perform at Hampton Institute, the women made plans for their families to go together. On the day of the performance, Dorothy looked over at her children, who were entranced by Anderson's beautiful voice. Dorothy knew this moment was one her family would never forget. She knew they were home.

9

BREAKING BARRIERS

Dorothy Vaughan and her husband saw each other on holidays and occasional weekends. They added two more children to their family, and for the younger ones, Newsome Park was the only home they knew. Dorothy loved staying home to take care of the new babies, but there was never a question that she would return to work as soon as possible after the children were old enough to stay with a babysitter. Dorothy's job at Langley provided the economic stability for the family.

While Dorothy and her children missed their family back in Farmville, friends from the West Computing office filled the void left by aunts and uncles and cousins. The group from West Computing began a summertime tradition of organizing a picnic at

Log Cabin Beach, a wooded resort over-looking the James River — a segregated beach built exclusively for black people. Dorothy preferred Log Cabin Beach to Bay-shore Beach in Hampton, where a rope divided Bayshore from whites-only Buckroe Beach next door. At Log Cabin, black families were able to enjoy being outside without "Colored" signs to remind them of their place.

Dorothy earned a good salary — $2,400 a year, twice the average monthly wage for black women in the 1940s. When the labo-ratory operated on a twenty-four-hour schedule during the war, Dorothy had worked the 3:00 p.m. to 11:00 p.m. shift, taking care of her family by day and crunch-ing numbers at night. Most of the other West Computers also decided to keep their jobs. The section had outgrown its original room in the Warehouse Building, and in 1945 they moved to two spacious offices on the first floor of the newly built Aircraft Loads Division building.

But providing for the needs of six children meant that vacations didn't come along often. Dorothy was frugal. She sewed clothes for herself and her children, clipped coupons, and wore shoes until her feet pushed through the worn soles.

She sacrificed for her children. Many evenings, Dorothy came home from work and made dinner for the family. After putting the meal on the table, she walked around the block until the children were done eating. She then ate only the leftovers. She didn't want to eat before she knew that her little ones had eaten all that they needed.

A Permanent Job

The prediction that the end of the war would destroy the economy of the Hampton Roads area proved incorrect. A defense industry boom followed the war and it lasted decades.

Hampton Roads became a military capital. After the war, the Norfolk Naval Base was established as the headquarters of the navy's air command. Next came the Army Transportation School in Newport News and the US Coast Guard base in Portsmouth. In 1946, the army decided to make Langley Field the headquarters of its Tactical Air Command. And then, the following year, the Army Air Corps became an independent branch of the military known as the United States Air Force.

The number of people working at Langley dropped immediately after the war. Most people left voluntarily, choosing to retire or take other work. Many women computers left to return home or marry men they had worked with. Engagement and wedding announcements filled the pages of the employee newsletter *Air Scoop.*

Another popular newsletter feature was "heir mail," a listing of birth announcements. The women had to figure out how to balance the demands of family and work on a long-term basis. Some women took time off to take care of their babies, while others quit their jobs altogether. But with the airplane growing ever more important to America's economy and its military, it seemed like Langley might always need talented computers.

In 1947, the laboratory disbanded the East Computing pool and sent the white women who had been working in that office to work in specific wind tunnels. All of East Computing's assignments were reassigned to West Computing. With the added work, West Computing remained in high gear. It wasn't surprising that Langley wanted to keep Dorothy Vaughan on as a computer. In three years she had proven herself by handing in error-free work and managing deadlines without complaint. She earned "excellent" ratings from her bosses and had been promoted to shift supervisor, managing one-third of a group that was now made up of twenty-five women.

Specialization

Men often came to the laboratory as junior engineers and were allowed to design and conduct their own experiments. Researchers took the men under their wings, teaching them the ropes. Women, on the other hand, had to work much harder to overcome other people's low expectations. A woman who worked in the central computing pool was one step removed from the research, and the engineers' assignments sometimes lacked the context to give the computer much knowledge about the project.

The work of most of the women was anonymous. Even a woman who had worked closely with an engineer on a research report rarely saw her name on the final publication. The engineers assumed it didn't matter; after all, she was just a woman, and many of the men were blind to the fact that a woman might have the same ambitions as a man.

Sometimes a computer's work impressed an engineer so much that he invited her to join him working full-time with a wind tunnel group. For the women, this meant an opportunity to get closer to the research,

By the 1960s, black and white women at Langley worked together on computing assignments. NASA-Langley.

and perhaps specialize in a particular subfield of aeronautics. A computer who could not only process data but also understand how to interpret it was more valuable to the team than a pool computer with more general knowledge. Specialization became the key to managing the increasingly complex nature of aeronautical research in the postwar era.

Sonic Boom

Many of the Langley engineers shared a dream: they wanted to design an aircraft capable of flying faster than the speed of sound. And the women at Langley were no exception. They dreamed of this exciting possibility, which was seeming less far-fetched by the day. To pursue this dream, in 1947, a group of thirteen employees, including two former East Computers, were sent to the Mojave Desert in the western part of the United States to establish a high-speed flight research center. Their mission: to build the fastest airplane in the world, one that could fly faster than the speed of sound.

The speed of sound is about 760 miles per hour. The exact number varies, depending on temperature, altitude, and humidity. Scientists used to think that flying faster than the speed of sound was impossible! But they were wrong.

"Mach 1" is the term for something moving at the speed of sound. When an object is moving this fast, the air molecules in front of the object can't get out of the way quickly enough, so they become compressed and form a shock wave. That shock wave is the noise we hear from the crack of a bullwhip or the firing of a bullet.

Scientists weren't sure what would happen to a pilot or his plane if he flew at Mach 1. Some researchers thought that the plane or the pilot would be destroyed by the power of the shock wave. Others disagreed.

There was only one way to find out: try it.

On October 14, 1947, pilot Chuck Yeager flew over the Mojave Desert in an NACA-developed experimental research plane called the Bell X-1. And he pierced the sound barrier for the first time in history! The plane caused a loud noise — a sonic boom, just like the shockwave from the bullet and the bullwhip — but the pilot and the plane were safe. The female computers on the ground verified the data transmitted from the instruments attached to the X-1 on its the record-breaking flight.

At the Mojave Desert facility, the computers who helped with this experiment had the chance to do significant work and get credit for it. They were promoted from "computer" to the higher position of "junior engineer," and were named as the authors of research reports, a necessary first step in the career of an engineer. And for a woman, it was an extraordinary achievement. It meant that the whole world would see that she had contributed to a worthy piece of research, and that she was an important member of an engineering team.

Dorothy Hoover, another black woman who worked in West Computing, was the first African-American woman to leave the computing pool and get a chance at a

Pilot Chuck Yeager stands next to the experimental aircraft Bell X-1, which he named Glamorous Glennis *after his wife.* US Air Force.

research job, working directly for an engineer. She had earned an undergraduate degree in math from Arkansas Agricultural, Mechanical & Normal College and a master's degree in mathematics from Atlanta University, and she taught in three states before coming to Langley in 1943. She was excellent at abstract concepts and complex equations. She had been assigned many of the most challenging problems and always submitted flawless work.

As a talented mathematician with an

independent mind, Dorothy Hoover was a perfect addition to any research team. Her visibility with engineers increased with her promotion. She answered the computers' questions and understood complex math so well that she sometimes knew more than many of the engineers in the lab.

The Section Leader

Dorothy Vaughan was an excellent leader within the West Area computing pool. In 1947, one of her bosses got sick and was out of the office for a month. The next year, the boss fell ill again. Then, in early 1949, Dorothy's boss began to act strangely at work. She suffered a mental breakdown and was forced to leave her job.

This tragic incident left the computing pool without a leader. But the engineers at the laboratory decided to choose Dorothy to be the temporary head of the entire section. This was the first time an African-American woman had been assigned a management role at Langley. At the time, it was unthinkable for a man to report to a woman. Men were always ultimately the people in charge. Women who had an interest in management were limited to heading a section in one of the computing pools or a division with female workers — but they always reported to a man. For Dorothy, the new job was a lot like being at the head of a high school classroom and reporting to a principal, who was usually a man.

It would take Dorothy Vaughan two years to earn the full title of "section head." The men she worked for held her in limbo: the laboratory had never had a black supervisor before, and they may have delayed making what seemed like a groundbreaking decision. Dorothy, however, was patient. Her promotion was made official when a memo circulated in January 1951: "Effective this date, Dorothy J. Vaughan, who has been acting head of West Area Computers unit, is hereby appointed head of that unit."

Dorothy took on the new responsibilities with confidence. Many of the women in West Computing knew she was the best candidate, and so did many engineers. In time her bosses realized it, too. History would prove them all right: there was no one better qualified for the job than Dorothy Vaughan.

Dorothy Vaughan after she retired from the National Aeronautics and Space Administration. The family of Dorothy J. Vaughan.

10

No Limits

In April 1951, a few months after Dorothy Vaughan became the boss of the West Area Computing pool, twenty-six-year-old Mary Winston Jackson came to work for her. Mary was new to the Langley Memorial Aeronautical Laboratory, but not new to the area. Mary and her family had deep roots in Hampton, Virginia. She grew up listening to the work songs of the black women shucking oysters at the processing plant in town. As a child, she heard elders at the black churches in town telling stories about sitting under a large oak tree across the river and listening to the Union soldiers read the Emancipation Proclamation, the edict issued by Abraham Lincoln in 1863, during the Civil War, which freed the slaves in the South.

Mary went to school in Hampton. In 1938, she graduated from Phenix High School with highest honors. She enrolled at Hampton Institute, where she pledged Alpha Kappa Alpha, the same black sorority that Dorothy Vaughan and many of the other West Computers had joined when they were in college.

Most of Hampton Institute's female students earned degrees in home economics or nursing, but Mary studied mathematics and physical science. After graduation she took a teaching job in Maryland. The following year, her father became sick, and she returned to Hampton to help care for him.

Back home, she took a position at a community center run by the United Services Organization (USO), a nonprofit group that provides services and entertainment to United States soldiers. She helped military families and defense workers find places to live, played the piano during sing-alongs, and helped organize Girl Scout troop meetings and rallies.

At one of the USO dances, Mary met Levi Jackson, an enlistee at the naval school run by the Hampton Institute. They fell in love and married in 1944. Always an independent-minded woman, Mary passed up the all-white bridal gown for a shorter white dress with black sequins, accessorized with black gloves, black pumps, and a red rose corsage. Mary Winston, now Mary Jackson, did things her own way.

Raising Expectations

When World War II ended, Levi Jackson found work as a painter at Langley Field. The USO closed, and Mary searched for a new job. She worked briefly as a bookkeeper but left after the birth of her son. For a while, she was a busy stay-at-home mom.

Even though taking care of her son kept her busy, Mary always found time for activities that made her happy. One of the things she loved the most was leading Girl Scout Troop 11, which was affiliated with her church. The organization's commitment to preparing women to take their place in the world with a mission of respect for God and country, and of honesty and loyalty, embodied Mary's core beliefs. She took the girls on three-mile hikes and field trips to the crab factory to learn more about what their parents did for work. She took them to an afternoon tea at the Hampton Institute Mansion House, where the college's president and his family lived. For the first time in history, Hampton Institute's president was black; the grand president's residence was occupied by a black family. It was a sight the girls never forgot: an impeccable black staff in a fabulous house, serving a black family.

Mary Jackson understood how impressionable the young girls were. At a troop meeting the group sang the folk tune "Pick a Bale of Cotton." It was a well-known song that she had sung countless times before, but that day it was as if she heard the words for the first time: "We're gonna jump down, turn around, pick a bale of cotton"! She realized it was talking about slavery times in the South, and she didn't want to keep that idea alive.

"Hold on a minute!" she interrupted. "We are never going to sing this again." She explained that the song reinforced all the worst stereotypes about what it meant to be black. She told the girls they could be much more than that.

Maybe Mary couldn't remove the limits that society put on the girls, but it was her duty to try to make sure the girls didn't put limits on themselves. Their dark skin, their gender, their economic status — none of these were reasons not to live out their dreams. You can do better; we can do better, she told them every day. For Mary Jackson, life was a long process of raising one's expectations.

Working at Langley

When her son turned four, Mary Jackson filled out an application with the Civil Service, applying both for a secretarial position and also for a job as a computer at Langley. In January 1951, she was hired as a secretary at Fort Monroe, an army base in Hampton. She was required to get a security clearance because of the documents she handled working for military officers.

Following World War II, the United States had become anxious about the threat posed by the Soviet Union. Though the two countries had been allies during the war, their relationship was less friendly, especially after the Soviet Union detonated its first atomic bomb. The United States and the Soviet Union didn't trust one another.

Then word spread that the Soviet Union had flown planes over Korea in 1950 that were "too fast to be identified." A headline in the 1950 *Norfolk Journal and Guide* read: "Russia Said to Have Fastest Fighter Plane." The United States had just assumed that it ruled the skies with its fast and powerful fleet of airplanes. After all, the country had led the way through the sound barrier with Chuck Yeager in 1947. By 1950, however, the NACA estimated that "the Russians expended at least three times the man power in their research establishments" compared to what the United States budgeted.

The National Advisory Committee on Aeronautics asked Congress for a larger budget, and eventually Langley started hiring again. The long list of job openings published in *Air Scoop* was similar to those of the boom time during the war. America had no intention of backing down or surrendering the skies to any other country.

Given Mary Jackson's background in mathematics, it came as no surprise that the government offered her a job working at Langley. Mary resigned from her job at the army base and went to work for Dorothy Vaughan.

No Speed Limits

The NACA engineers had successfully broken the sound barrier, but they knew that in order to stay ahead of the Russians, they had to build even faster planes; not just experimental aircraft, but ones that could be put into production for the military. "For America to continue its present challenged supremacy in the air will require that it develop tactical military aircraft that will fly faster than sound before any other nation does so," the NACA's executive secretary said in the *Norfolk Journal and Guide.* Mach 1 was just the beginning — engineers and pilots dreamed of flying with no speed limits. Some engineers imagined a day when pilots could fly at Mach 5 or faster — 3,800 miles per hour! The laboratory built new wind tunnels, capable of conducting research at velocities from below the speed of sound up to Mach 7 — a tunnel so fast it was labeled hypersonic. The engineers and mathematicians like Dorothy and Mary sharpened their pencils and got to work to try to figure out how to send humans flying through the air at speeds that even a decade before would have been unimaginable.

The Communist Threat

On April 5, 1951, the same day that Mary Jackson started her job at Langley, a New York federal court handed down a death sentence against Ethel and Julius Rosenberg, a couple accused of spying for the Russians. The Rosenberg trial sparked widespread fears that communist sympathizers — people who believed in Communism, Russia's political system — were living inside the United States and plotting

The Hypersonic Wind Tunnel Complex at Langley Memorial Aeronautics Laboratory in Hampton, Virginia. **NASA-Langley.**

to overthrow the American government.

At Langley, the Rosenberg trial and its repercussions hit close to home. An engineer was accused of stealing classified National Advisory Committee for Aeronautics documents and giving them to the Soviet Union. Some of the stolen secrets included plans for a nuclear-powered airplane and designs for parts of a high-speed aircraft. The engineer was eventually cleared of spying charges, but he was convicted of lying about

*Ethel and Julius Rosenberg were American citizens
accused of spying for the Soviet Union. They were
tried and convicted, and were executed in 1953.*
United States Library of Congress.

his relationship with the Rosenbergs.

Suddenly, Americans were afraid that
there might be spies all around them, even
in their neighborhoods or at work. The FBI
interviewed Langley employees. Many
workers were terrified of the investigators,
who sometimes came to their homes unan-
nounced. While no one was above suspicion,
the investigators focused their attention on

anyone involved with organizations that the government had decided were dangerous.

The FBI accused people involved with many organizations of being sympathetic to the communists and their beliefs. The fear of Communism ruined many lives and livelihoods, even when people were innocent.

Virginia's senator Harry Byrd, the same politician who had criticized the Fair Employment Practices laws from World War II, stirred up another frenzy by labeling anyone who disagreed with his view of "traditional" American values as a Communist.

But President Harry S. Truman saw a different way to deal with Communism. He wanted to show that the United States' version of democracy was the best system in the world, encouraging developing countries, including many in Africa, Asia, and Latin America, to become American allies. To prove that America was trying to be more fair to people with dark skin, President Truman desegregated the military, allowing blacks and whites to serve side by side in the armed forces. Truman also made the head of each federal department "personally responsible" for maintaining a work environment free of discrimination on the basis of race, color, religion, or national origin.

Was discrimination taking place at Langley? On the one hand, the black women were still racially segregated into the West Computing office. "The laboratory has one work unit composed entirely of Negro women, the West Area Computers, which may fall into the category of a segregated work unit," wrote one of Langley's administrative officers in a 1951 memo. "However," the memo continued, "a large percentage of employees are usually detailed to work in non-segregated units for periods of one to three months." Over time, women like Dorothy Hoover — West Computing's other Dorothy — had begun to leave the computing pool and go to work in other offices, sitting next to white engineers and computers. The women knew that the best way to fight discrimination at work was to do their work as well as they possibly could. The mathematical equations didn't care what color they were, as long as the answers were correct.

11

THE AREA RULE

In the early 1950s, Dorothy Vaughan and the women working in the West Computing office were always busy. Most days, they worked in their own office, but sometimes other groups at the laboratory asked Dorothy to send one of her mathematicians over to their offices when the engineers needed extra help. One day, a group on the East Side asked for help, and Dorothy decided to send Mary Jackson. Mary went over to the new office, where she was to work with several white computers.

Since Mary's office was on the West Side, she wasn't familiar with all of the buildings on the East Side. At some point during the day, she needed a break and asked her coworkers, "Can you direct me to the bathroom?"

They giggled. How would *they* know where to find *her* bathroom?

The nearest women's bathroom was open to the white women but not to Mary, because she was black. There were "colored" bathrooms somewhere on the East Side, but Mary didn't know where. She stormed off to look on her own.

Negotiating racial boundaries was a daily task for African Americans. Mary was used to it, but something about the incident really bothered her. She was just as smart and just as talented as her coworkers. The Langley employee badge supposedly gave Mary access to the same workplace as her white coworkers. She came to work with the same education, maybe even more. She dressed each day as if she were on her way to a meeting with the president. She was a professional.

Mary Jackson was angered — no, enraged — to have been confronted with such blatant prejudice in a workplace dedicated to scientific and rational thought, and she considered it absurd to be singled out for something as common and universal as going to the bathroom. In the moment that her white coworkers laughed at her, Mary had been demoted from professional mathematician to second-class human being.

An Unexpected Offer

Still angry as she walked back to West Computing later that day, Mary Jackson ran into the assistant section head at the 4-foot by 4-foot Supersonic Pressure Tunnel (4-foot SPT), a powerful wind tunnel located on the West Side. Most African Americans were automatically careful about how they spoke around whites, wearing a mask that kept them from saying what they really meant. Mary let her mask slip when the engineer asked her how she was doing. Unable to control her anger, she let off steam and ranted about the insulting way she had been treated by the women that morning.

Mary was a soft-spoken person, but she was also direct and forthright. She was a good judge of character, and she sensed that she could trust the engineer. She picked the right person to talk to. He didn't think her feelings were unreasonable or unjustified.

"Why don't you come work for me?" he asked. He respected her as a person and admired her work as a mathematician. He knew she would be an asset to his team.

Mary accepted his offer.

She transferred over to his research team, working with the SPT, one of the best tunnels for testing airplanes flying faster than the speed of sound.

Mary Jackson, first row, far right, in a group photo of the Supersonic Pressure Tunnel Group at the Langley Memorial Aeronautical Laboratory. NASA-Langley.

Theoretical Engineers

While a great deal of attention was placed on the air tunnels and test flights, Langley wasn't a bad place for theoretical engineers, either. A theoretical engineer is someone who works with numbers and papers, designing aircraft based on ideas or theories, rather than using experiments and testing. Dorothy Hoover, who had started working in West Computinng the same year as Dorothy Vaughan, continued to thrive in her division, earning the title of "aeronautical research scientist," a high ranking for a woman of any color. In 1951, she published two reports, both detailed analyses of the swept-back wings that were now standard in aircraft. What the wind-tunnel and fresh-air engineers examined through direct observation, the theoreticians approached through complex math. They prepared fifty-page papers where a single equation might take up most of an entire page.

Dorothy Hoover and at least three other women working in this group published research reports between 1947 and 1951. The group leaders clearly valued and cultivated the talent of its female members. In 1952, Dorothy Hoover decided to take a leave of absence from engineering to go back to school. She resigned from Langley and returned to academic life at Arkansas Agricultural, Mechanical & Normal College, where she earned a master's degree in mathematics.

Mary Jackson, on the other hand, threw herself into her work with her engineering team. She loved rolling up her sleeves and working with airplane models so she could understand the physical phenomena behind the calculations she worked on. Like many other former computers, she was on her way to becoming a Langley "lifer," someone who stayed with the agency for her entire career.

The Numbers Don't Lie

Soon after becoming a mathematician with the Supersonic Pressure Tunnel, Mary Jackson was given an assignment by her boss's boss's boss, a division chief, one of the laboratory's top-ranking managers and most respected researchers. He gave her instructions for working through a set of calculations. She did the work and delivered the finished assignment after double-checking her results.

Something didn't seem right to the manager who assigned the work. He insisted that Mary's calculations were wrong.

Mary Jackson respectfully stood by her work.

Mary and the division chief reviewed the numbers and finally discovered that the problem wasn't with her output but with his input: he had given her the wrong numbers to use! Based on those numbers, Mary's calculations were indeed correct. When they realized the mistake, he apologized to her. Mary's willingness to stand by her work earned her a reputation around the office as a smart and dedicated mathematician.

Most engineers were good mathematicians, but for the most part it was the women who knew how to work with the numbers. They were the experts. They checked each other's work and put red dots on the data sheets when they found errors. There were very, very few red dots.

Some of the women were capable of lightning-fast mental math. Others had a highly refined understanding of theoretical math. The best of the women made names for themselves for accuracy, speed, and insight. But having the independence of mind and strength of personality to defend your work in front of the most powerful aeronautical minds in the world — that's what got you noticed. That's what marked you as someone who should move ahead. That was Mary Jackson.

Mary Jackson after retiring from her work with the
National Aeronautics and Space Administration.
NASA-Langley.

12

An Exceptional Mind

Like Mary Jackson, Katherine Goble was a gifted mathematician who put her talents to work as a teacher. She was quite content with her life as a wife and mother, teaching math and French in Marion, Virginia. It would be years before she learned of the work being done at the NACA in Hampton. But everything would change in August 1952, when she attended a family wedding.

At the wedding, Katherine's husband's brother-in-law told Katherine that the government was hiring black women to work as mathematicians at Langley. He knew she had studied mathematics in college and graduate school. He was the director of the Newsome Park Community Center, where Dorothy Vaughan and her family lived. He knew Dorothy had quite a few of the women working for her in West Computing,

Katherine listened carefully. She and her husband were public school teachers with modest paychecks. They had three daughters and had to manage their budget carefully to cover all of their family's needs. She enjoyed teaching and felt a sense of responsibility to "advance the race" by giving her students the best possible education, even though they attended segregated schools with fewer resources. But now, the mention of the opportunity at Langley reminded her of something she had almost forgotten: the dream of being a professional mathematician. After many years, it looked as if that dream just might come true.

A Mind for Math

Katherine's father was a math whiz. Though educated only through the sixth grade, he could tell how much lumber a tree would yield just by looking at it. From the time she was a toddler, Katherine's parents realized that she had inherited her father's mind for math. Katherine, the youngest of four children, counted whatever crossed her path — dishes, steps, and stars in the sky. She excelled in school, especially in math. Whenever her teachers noticed that Katherine's desk was empty, they would look for her in the classroom next door, where they would find her helping her older brother with his math lesson.

Katherine graduated from high school at age fourteen. In 1933, she enrolled at West Virginia State Institute, a black college outside Charleston. By her junior year, she had tackled every math course the school offered, so her math professor created special advanced math classes just for her.

"You would make a good research mathematician," her professor told Katherine when she was a sophomore. "I am going to prepare you for this career." He believed in Katherine and her special ability, even though job prospects were poor. In the 1930s, employers openly discriminated against Irish and Jewish women with math degrees; the odds of a black woman finding work as a mathematician were especially low.

After graduation, Katherine took a job teaching at the high school in Marion, Virginia. She met Jimmy Goble and they fell in love and married, but they kept their marriage secret. Katherine loved teaching, but at the time, the law didn't allow married women in the classroom as teachers.

"Unusually Capable"

In the spring of 1940, at the end of a busy school day, Katherine was surprised to find the president of her former college waiting outside her classroom. He said he had a special opportunity for her. Because no graduate programs were offered at any black colleges in the state, the all-white West Virginia University could be forced to admit African Americans to their graduate programs in order to comply with a Supreme Court Order. If a state didn't operate a separate graduate school for black students, it would be required to integrate its existing graduate schools. Since there were no graduate programs for black students in the entire state of West Virginia, the law said that the white school had to open its doors to blacks.

The governor of West Virginia didn't want to fight the law. Instead, he planned to integrate the state's public graduate schools. He asked for the names of three "unusually capable" West Virginia State College graduates who might be willing to desegregate the university. Katherine was asked to be one of the three. (The other two were men who would be entering the law school.)

Katherine accepted a place in the graduate school studying mathematics. On her last day teaching at the high school, Katherine's principal presented her with a full set of math reference books. He wanted her to succeed and he feared that, as one of the school's first black students, she might have trouble accessing the books she needed at the white school's library.

Katherine enrolled in West Virginia University's summer session. Her mother moved to Morgantown, West Virginia, to room with her daughter, hoping to help her navigate what could be a difficult situation if the white students chose to bully her or call her names. As it turned out, most of the white students welcomed Katherine, and some went out of their way to be friendly. Only one classmate gave her any trouble, and that student just tried to insult Katherine by ignoring her. The professors treated her fairly, and Katherine more than met the academic standard. Her greatest challenge: finding a course that didn't repeat what she had already learned.

At the end of the summer session, Katherine found that she and her husband were expecting a baby. Being quietly married was one thing, but having a baby was another. Katherine and her husband announced the news to her family, who were overjoyed, although they realized that she was going to have to leave school.

Katherine became a full-time wife and mother; she and Jimmy eventually had three daughters. She never regretted putting family life ahead of graduate school. In 1944, Katherine took a teaching job at the local black high school to help support her family. She remained at that job until she learned about the opportunity at Langley in 1952.

A New Life

After listening to their brother-in-law describe the job at Langley, Katherine and her husband, Jimmy, decided to take the leap and move to Newport News. When they arrived, they moved into an apartment in Newsome Park. Her husband got a stable, well-paid job as a painter at the Newport News shipyard. Their three children loved their new school and marveled at being part of such a large and dynamic black community.

Langley's personnel department approved Katherine's job application as a computer in 1952, but she didn't start work until June 1953. In the meantime she worked as a substitute math teacher at the high school, which allowed her to meet a lot of families in the area. She was involved with her sorority and her church. She developed a social network and met the woman who would become a lifelong best friend, Eunice Smith, who lived three blocks away and was a nine-year veteran at West Computing.

When Katherine started work, she and Eunice decided drive to the office together. It was a great surprise for Katherine to find not only that her new boss, Dorothy Vaughan, was a fellow West Virginian, but that their families had once been neighbors. It didn't take long for Katherine to appreciate that Dorothy wasn't just a talented mathematician — she was also a great supervisor.

For two weeks, Katherine worked at her new desk in West Computing, hitting the ground running. Then one morning, an engineer came into the office and quietly conferred with Dorothy. "The Flight Research Division needs two new computers," Dorothy Vaughan announced. The Flight Research Division was a group that specialized in testing real planes, rather than wind tunnels. "Katherine and Erma, I'm sending the two of you," assigning Katherine and another West Computer to the job.

Confusing Signals

For Katherine, being given an assignment in the Flight Research Division, whose office was on the top floor of Langley's gigantic hangar, felt like good fortune. She had been elated to work in the pool and calculate her way through the data sheets, but being sent to work closely with the engineers was even more exciting.

With just her lunch bag and purse to carry, Katherine went over to the hanger, which was a short walk from the West Computing office. She slipped in the side door, climbed the stairs, and walked down a dim cinder block hallway to the Flight Research Laboratory. Inside, the room smelled like coffee and cigarettes — the engineers smoked and drank coffee all day while they were working.

Like West Computing, the office was set up in classroom style with about twenty desks. Most of the people on the team were men, but there were a few other women in the group, working as computers. Katherine looked for a place to wait for her new bosses. She went to an empty cube and sat down next to a white engineer.

Before she had a chance to say hello, the man gave her a sideways glance, then got up and walked away.

Had she done something wrong? No one else noticed what happened, but Katherine didn't know whether his action was meant to be insulting.

It could have been because she was black and he was white.

It could have been because she was a woman and he was a man.

It could have been because he was a professional and she was a subprofessional.

Or it could have meant nothing at all.

Outside the Langley campus, the rules were clear. Blacks and whites lived separately, ate separately, studied separately, socialized separately, worshipped separately, and, for the most part, worked separately. At Langley, the boundaries were fuzzy.

Some of her colleagues were Northerners or foreigners who'd never so much as met a black person before arriving at Langley. Others were from the Deep South, with strong attitudes about racial mixing. It was all a part of the racial relations laboratory at Langley. Blacks and whites were exploring new ground together.

Katherine and the other black mathematicians mounted a charm offensive: they made a special effort to always be well-dressed, well-spoken, patriotic, and upright. They were keenly aware that the interactions that individual blacks had with whites could have implications for the entire black community.

Within two weeks, whatever had caused the engineer to move away from Katherine's desk had faded from mind as the two got to know one another. The man was more than pleased when he discovered that his new office mate was a fellow transplant from West Virginia, and they became fast friends. West Virginia never left Katherine's heart, but Virginia, it would soon be clear, was her destiny.

13

TURBULENCE

After six months, Katherine Goble's temporary assignment to the Flight Research Division was starting to look permanent. At the beginning of 1954, Dorothy Vaughan sat down with Katherine's boss in the division. "Either give her a raise or send her back to me," Dorothy said.

Although Katherine had spent only two weeks in the West Area computing office when she first arrived at Langley, she was still Dorothy's responsibility. The way Dorothy saw the matter, Katherine should either be classified as a permanent member of West Computing and continue to rotate through other temporary assignments, or she should become an official member of the Flight Research Division.

Even though the manager Katherine reported to was not an advocate of women in the workforce, the meeting ended as both the manager and Dorothy Vaughan knew it would: Katherine received an offer to join the division full time, with an increase in salary.

The engineers who worked with Katherine realized that she was a keeper soon after she showed them her mathematical skills. Her familiarity with higher-level math made her a versatile addition to the branch.

The Flight Research Division was a collection of high-energy, free-thinking, aggressive, and very smart engineers. They spent their time not in the wind tunnels but with live aircraft. They were serious about their work; the head of the Flight Research Division had actually trained as a test pilot in order to improve the quality of his research reports. The division was the kind of place that would not show patience to anyone — male or female — who took too long to figure out how things were supposed to be done.

Fortunately, Katherine Goble's natural curiosity and her confidence in her own mathematical ability gave her the courage to ask the engineers a lot of questions. They didn't hesitate to explain what they knew. They spent a good part of their lives thinking about flight, and they could talk about it endlessly.

Branches within the Flight Research Division investigated different topics, such as planes that could travel faster than the speed of sound and even ones that might be capable of flying into outer space. One of the tasks of the Maneuver Loads Branch, where Katherine worked, was to examine safety concerns and investigate plane crashes.

A Bumpy Ride

Katherine's first assignment in the group was to help figure out what went wrong in an accident involving a small Piper propeller plane. The plane, which was flying along in an unremarkable fashion, literally fell out of the clear blue sky and crashed without apparent cause. The National Advisory Committee for Aeronautics received the plane's flight recorder — a device that tracks an aircraft's speed, acceleration, altitude, and other measures of flight. The information was essential to figuring out what had happened.

It was Katherine's job to analyze the photographic images of the plane's instruments, recorded in very small increments of time. Hour after hour, day after day, she looked through a film reader, studying what was happening to the plane before the crash. She learned that the propeller plane flew in a path perpendicular to that of a larger jet plane that had passed through the area a few minutes before. The engineers set up an experiment, re-creating the circumstances of the accident, flying a test plane into the trailing wake of a larger plane. The data from that experiment also arrived on Katherine's desk. It was eye-straining, monotonous computer work, but Katherine loved it.

When the engineers analyzed Katherine's work, they were fascinated to recognize something they hadn't realized before. The data showed that the air disturbance caused by a jet that flew past could trouble the air for as long as a half hour after it had passed through. This wave of air had tripped up the smaller propeller plane as it flew through it, causing it to stumble and crash. This was a revelation, and Katherine was thrilled to be a part of the team that uncovered it.

The research done by Katherine and the engineers on the team led to changes in air traffic regulations, requiring minimum distances between flight paths to prevent similar accidents. Katherine thought that report was "one of the most interesting

This experiment carried out by the Langley Research Center used colored smoke rising from the ground to make visible the air flow, or turbulence, from the wing during flight. **NASA-Langley.**

things [she] had ever read." She also felt satisfied to have helped with such an important project.

From the beginning, Katherine felt at home at Langley. She took a genuine liking to her new colleagues, who were opinionated, high energy, and interesting. Best of all, as far as Katherine was concerned, they were smart as whips.

Like other black people, Katherine was

aware that discrimination existed at Langley, just as it existed in other areas of life. But she made the decision to block it out of her daily routine. She refused to allow herself to worry about it too much. When she first took the job, she didn't realize the bathrooms were segregated. Not every building had a "colored" bathroom and the ones for the white women were unmarked. As far as Katherine was concerned, there was no reason why she shouldn't use the unmarked bathrooms as well.

The Next Challenge

After they'd been living in Newsome Park for two years, Katherine's husband said, "I want to move our girls out of the projects." Living in the subdivision when they first arrived in town had made it possible for the family to become a part of the black community in the area very quickly, but they decided to move to Mimosa Crescent, a World War II–era neighborhood in Hampton that had been built for middle-class black families. In 1946, Mimosa Crescent had more than doubled in size, growing from its original twenty-two houses to fifty-one. The area attracted more prosperous families who were able to afford the three- and four-bedroom brick houses.

With a lovely new home, a job she loved, and her three daughters all doing well in school, Katherine felt she was living the American dream — at least for a while. Then, over the course of 1955, her husband began to feel sick, first with headaches, then with unexplained weakness. Ultimately, his doctors discovered a tumor at the base of his skull, where it could not be treated.

His health declined over more than a year, and much of that time he was in the hospital. Katherine's husband, James Francis Goble, died five days before Christmas in 1956.

Katherine was devastated, of course. But she refused to give in to her grief. She had made a promise to her husband that she would do everything in her power to keep their bright, lively daughters on the path that they had paved for them. Katherine allowed herself and the girls until the end of the year to mourn, and then she expected them all to get back to work.

On the first day of school in January 1957, Katherine met with the school principal. "It is very important that you don't show the girls any special treatment, or let up on them in any way," she said. "They are going to college, and they need to be prepared."

Now that she was a single mother, Katherine established the new household rules. "You will have my clothes ironed and ready in the morning, and dinner ready when I come home," she told her daughters. Katherine was now both mother and father, the one who offered love and discipline, the sole breadwinner. Each of them would have to work hard to pull the family through the difficult time.

The Goble children excelled in school; they took piano and violin lessons and practiced diligently. They were good-natured, outgoing, and respectful. With her steady gaze on the future, Katherine led her daughters toward the long-promised blessings of democracy. She wasn't leading the life she had expected, but she accepted the new challenges with dignity.

Katherine's husband's death divided her life in two. As a couple, they had walked side by side through graduate school and marriage, the birth of their children, and their move to Newport News. Now, at just thirty-eight years old, she was a widow and a single mother, as well as a professional woman realizing her intellectual dream. Her husband wouldn't be there to see those dreams come to fruition, but he had helped get her career launched. All that had come before would connect to all that was to come. In January 1957, Katherine's daughters went back to school and she went back to work: the second act of her life was about to begin.

14

PROGRESS

The years after World War II were an age of technological progress. Jet engines replaced propellers. Reaching Mach 1 left engineers hungry to conquer Mach 2. Supersonic flight led to still-faster hypersonic flight.

Each breakthrough pushed the imaginations of inventors and engineers a little bit further, tempting the workers at the Langley Memorial Aeronautics Laboratory to envision a time when they eventually would create an aircraft capable of breaking free of Earth's gravity and reaching outer space.

One step in this march of progress had occurred in 1947 when Langley bought its first "electronic calculator" from Bell Telephone Laboratories. No one confused the female calculators with the room-sized calculating machines that performed the same function. As the years passed and the electronic computers became more important to the work done at Langley, Dorothy Vaughan could envision a time when her team of human computers would be replaced by the inanimate calculating machines. The future was coming. Dorothy didn't know exactly what the new computers would look like, but she knew that technology was going to change the way things were done at the laboratory.

The New Machines

The electronic calculators were needed for the more elaborate research being carried out by the National Advisory Committee for Aeronautics. As planes flew faster than the speed of sound, the math required to study those supersonic flights had become increasingly complicated. Some of the algebraic equations the mathematicians were asked to perform had as many as thirty-five variables and might take as long as a month to solve. The new electronic calculator could complete the same problem in just a few hours!

These computers were fast, but they weren't easy to use. The machines used paper punch tapes — long strips of paper with holes punched out to store data — as input and chugged along at two seconds per math operation (like addition or subtraction). The whole building shook when the machine was in use, but it offered the distinct advantage that it could operate all night long. The female computers needed to go home to rest.

A New Era

In the mid-1950s, the National Advisory Committee for Aeronautics bought its first computers from IBM, an IBM 604 Electronic Calculating Punch and an IBM 650. The engineers needed them to calculate the flight path for a hypersonic (above Mach 5) "rocket plane," an experimental aircraft that would fly high enough and fast enough to leave Earth's atmosphere and break the pull of Earth's gravity in order to reach space.

At first, these data-processing machines weren't very reliable. They made mistakes, and engineers — or the human computers who worked for the engineers — had to keep an eye on the output.

In the 1950s, the electronic computers with their million-dollar-plus price tags were only used by large research facilities. They were fast, but they could still process just one job at a time. They chugged out answers around the clock, but competition for computing time remained fierce. Every engineer wanted time on the machines.

Only the most shortsighted of the human computers failed to see that the electronic computers were going to dominate the future. The machines brought vast amounts of computing power and efficiency to the research process. Evolution occurred in scientific progress just as it does in nature: positive traits continued and obsolete ones died off. For example, propeller research had been one of Langley's most important areas of investigation at one time, but the propeller plans were replaced by faster jet engines. By 1951, the propeller tunnel was declared obsolete and demolished. Engineers who had staffed it were left to find a new specialty or retire.

The same thing was going to be true of the human computers. They would have to evolve or they would become obsolete. The machines didn't immediately threaten the mathematicians' jobs, but Dorothy Vaughan realized that mastering the electronic calculators would be the key to job security. When Langley started giving classes in computer programming after work and on weekends, she signed up. And she encouraged the women in her group to do the same.

Dorothy knew there would be more direct and open competition with the white computers, and African-American women had to meet — or exceed — the standards. But she expected that those new jobs would be open to her and the other computers if they were ready. "Integration is going to come," she said. She recognized that the blurring of the color lines could put her and her team in a position to qualify for the desirable jobs that were going to open up for people who were experts in managing the electronic computers. To keep moving forward, African-American women needed to take advantage of every opportunity for additional training.

Dorothy attended all the classes on computer programming that she could find. Langley offered a series of after-work lectures on aerodynamics there at the laboratory. Other classes were offered at Hampton Institute, the Langley Air Force Base, the College of William and Mary, and Newport News High School.

Hampton High School was the seat of the University of Virginia's Extension School, one of Langley's campuses. In the evenings, Langley's top researchers taught classes to laboratory employees at the city's only public high school, but the high school was off-limits to the city's African-American children, who were sent to Phenix High School, on the campus of Hampton Institute.

School segregation had become a red-hot topic across the country. Politicians and ordinary citizens debated the quality of its schools, especially how American students compared to Soviet students in math and science. The goal of raising the general level of technical proficiency had only grown stronger as the rift between the United States and the Soviet Union intensified. The fear of Communism and spies had exploded during the period that became known as the Cold War.

In the United States, the debate had expanded into a broader discussion of the participation of African Americans in the technical fields. If the United States wanted to cultivate the best and brightest students in math and science, why waste the much-needed brainpower of black children by sending them to inferior schools? Every day, Katherine Goble, Dorothy Vaughan, Mary Jackson, and other Langley computers were proving that women were as good at math as men, and that African Americans were just as gifted at math as anyone else.

A Woman Engineer

Mary Jackson was putting her math skills to good use in her new job.

From the beginning of her assignment in the wind tunnel research section, Mary's new boss, Kazimierz Czarnecki, had shown Mary how to work the controls of their wind tunnel for her group, firing up the tunnel's roaring engine and positioning models in the test section. The research in her division was used to design missiles, which were of great interest to the United States government for their possible military use. In its final form, her work became the 1958 report coauthored with her boss, "Effects on Nose Angle and Mach Number on Transition on Cones at Supersonic Speeds."

Mary's new boss was so impressed with her work that he suggested she enroll in Langley's engineer training program. Her ability and passion were apparent, and she had a mentor — her boss — who believed in her. It didn't matter that Mary was black and Kaz was white. It didn't matter that Mary was a woman and Kaz was a man. It didn't matter that Mary was from the South and Kaz was from the North. What mattered was that they both loved math, and they both loved airplanes. Kaz knew that Mary had the talent to be an engineer.

At the time, there were very few white women who worked as engineers. The majority of Langley's female professionals, black and white, were still classified as computers or mathematicians. There simply weren't many female engineers anywhere in the country. At the time, most of the country's top engineering schools didn't accept women. The only female engineer at Langley in the mid-1950s — Kitty O'Brien Joyner — had to sue the University of Virginia in order to enroll in the undergraduate engineering school in 1939.

There were also very few African-American men who worked as engineers. Mary was on her way to becoming something even rarer: an African-American woman working as an engineer. In 1952, Howard University had had only two female engineering graduates in the school's history. In fact, Mary was on track to become the first female African-American engineer at Langley.

Mary's boss put her on the engineering track and promised her a promotion when she successfully completed a few advanced math courses. When she went to enroll in her courses, the obstacle she encountered came not from her coworkers but from the local high school. Before she could get any training, Mary had to get permission to enter Hampton High School. If she had been the janitor, she would have been welcomed. As a professional engineer-in-training, she had to petition the City of Hampton for "special permission" to attend classes in the whites-only school.

Mary Jackson had to grit her teeth and take a deep breath before making the case to the school board that she should be allowed to attend the classes at Hampton High School. She reminded herself that she had a long-term goal, and she didn't want to get sidetracked. So she swallowed her pride and asked for permission, which the City of Hampton granted.

The Disappointment of Hampton High School

Mary Jackson had passed the old Hampton High School too many times to count. The building was located in the middle of the city, not far from her house, but she had never set foot inside. On her first night of class, in the spring of 1956, Mary was nervous. Her classmates were the same people she had worked with during the day for the past five years, but she was anxious about meeting with them outside of the Langley campus.

The thought of entering the whites-only school also worried Mary. Nothing could have prepared her for the shock she experienced when she walked through the door. Hampton High School was a dilapidated, musty old building.

Mary Jackson was stunned. *This* was what she and the rest of the black children in the city had been denied all these years? She had assumed that if whites had worked so hard to deny her admission to the school, it must have been a beautiful place. But this?

What a nonsensical thing that black and whites went to different schools! If the city had combined its resources, it could have built one beautiful school for both black and white students. Throughout the South, cities had maintained two separate and inefficient school systems, which shortchanged both black and white students.

Pioneers

Being on the leading edge of the battle over integration was not for the faint of heart. Mary Jackson was friends with Thomas Byrdsong, a black engineer who had come to Langley in 1952. Mary's husband, Levi, was an excellent cook, and Thomas Byrdsong loved going to the Jacksons' house for dinner. The friends laughed and talked, often discussing work, and enjoyed Levi's meals.

As a recent graduate of the University of Michigan, Byrdsong had been assigned to a senior engineer in a wind tunnel division. His boss instructed him on how to conduct his first test, then assigned him a partner — a mechanic — to assist and answer questions. The mechanic, a white man with years of experience at the lab, sabotaged Byrdsong's first experiment by incorrectly attaching the model during the test. Byrdsong knew he had been undermined, but he didn't say anything. He was from the South and knew all too well that many people would defend a white man over a black man in any kind of dispute.

When Byrdsong presented his data, his boss recognized that he had been sabotaged and was irate. "You will never do that again to this man or anyone else. Do you understand me?" the boss shouted at the mechanic.

Byrdsong went out of his way to remain calm at work, but keeping his anger bottled up wasn't good for him, either. In general, black men at Langley were more likely to have trouble over racial issues than black women. Their good manners and gracious attitudes did not always protect them.

Though the white engineers were typically polite and respectful to the black men, it was often the blue-collar mechanics, model makers, and technicians who were threatened and made the African Americans feel unwelcome.

For Thomas Byrdsong, the constant battle against race wore him down. Like Katherine Goble, he found a way to opt out of the segregated facilities. Each day at lunchtime he and a friend escaped to a black-owned restaurant just outside the entrance to the air force base. There he could be himself.

Ultimately, Thomas Byrdsong, Mary Jackson, and each of the other African Americans at Langley had to navigate race relations in their own way. The challenges facing black employees at the laboratory reflected the similar conflicts happening all over the country. The civil rights movement was gaining strength, and African Americans nationwide were trying to establish their rights and freedoms in the classrooms, in the voting booths, and in the halls of Congress, where legislative reforms were being considered.

On the world stage, chilly relations between the United States and the Soviet Union kept everyone uneasy. The two world powers were vying for control of Earth and outer space, challenging one another politically and technologically. Each country wanted to demonstrate its scientific prowess and dominate the skies. The world was on the cusp of making new discoveries that would allow mankind to experience outer space. There was one central question: Who would get there first?

15

YOUNG, GIFTED, AND BLACK

While Mary Jackson was busy at work helping the NACA build supersonic airplanes, girls in high school were beginning to imagine different possibilities for themselves. Even though teaching was still the best option available, there were now more career choices.

On October 5, 1957, Christine Mann, a senior at the Allen School for girls in Asheville, North Carolina, left her dorm room first thing in the morning and walked to the library. Her job was to open the library and organize the newspapers and magazines before anyone else arrived. She took a moment to read the headlines as she set up the displays.

Since the beginning of the school year, newspapers around the country had discussed the racial crisis in Little Rock, Arkansas: nine black teenagers trying to integrate the all-white Central High School had turned that state's capital city into a military battleground. The Arkansas National Guard had been called out to prevent the black students from entering the school. In response, the federal government sent US Army troops to escort the nine students into the school. The crisis unfolded over days, and each morning Christine followed the news of the brave children who were close to her in age.

The showdown had dominated the headlines — and then the Soviet Union launched *Sputnik.* The Russians did it — they had created a satellite and launched it into orbit — and they did it before the United States. With tensions between the two countries already high because of the Cold War, this news put everyone further on edge. The United States needed to catch up!

At the Langley Memorial Aeronautics Laboratory, there was great pressure to outperform the Russians at 360 miles above Earth, the altitude at which a satellite would fly around the planet. For the engineers, beating the Russians in space was a matter of personal and professional pride.

In the rest of the country, the fear was

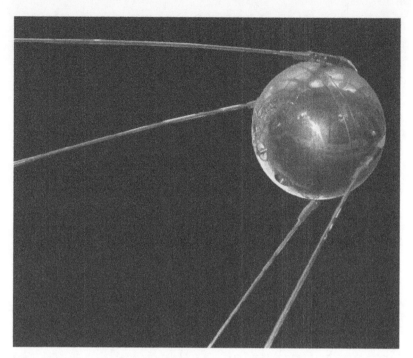

A replica of the Soviet Union's Sputnik 1, *the first artificial satellite to be put into outer space.* Courtesy of the National Air and Space Museum and NASA.

political. "Red-Made Satellite Flashes Across US," read the *Daily Press* in Newport News. "Sphere Tracked in 4 Crossings over US," read the *New York Times.*

When Christine read the news, she felt she had fallen asleep in one world and awakened in another. October 4, 1957, marked the end of the postwar era, a time when the world was rebuilding after the destruction of World War II. The morning of October 5 was the official dawn of the space age, the beginning of mankind's realizing a long-held dream to fly beyond Earth's atmosphere and visit outer space.

President Dwight D. Eisenhower tried to dismiss the Russians' "small ball in the air" as an insignificant achievement, but the American people knew better. *Sputnik,* some experts declared, was nothing less than a technological declaration of war. The Russians had won the first battle, but the space race was just getting started.

The *Sputnik* Age
For the third time in the century, the United States found itself falling behind other countries technologically during a period of international tension. On the cusp of World War I, the country didn't have enough airplanes, so the government created the National Advisory Committee for Aeronautics. At the start of World War II, America's aircraft industry lagged behind Germany's, but during the war it surged to global dominance. Now the threat came from the Soviet Union.

It wasn't just *Sputnik.* The Soviet Union had missiles — perhaps hundreds of them — with the power to reach US cities and deliver nuclear bombs. A new term began to make the rounds in policy circles, the press, and private conversations: the "missile gap."

Black newspapers and their readers wasted no time in making the link between America's inadequacy in space and the dreadful conditions facing many black students in the South. "While we were forming mobs to drive Autherine Lucy [the black woman who integrated the University of Alabama in 1956] from the Alabama campus, the Russians were compelling ALL children to attend the best possible schools," argued the *Chicago Defender.* Until the United States changed its views on racial inequality and gave the same opportunities to all students, it would never be able to lead the world, the newspaper commented.

An editorial in the Cleveland *Call and Post* echoed that idea: "Who can say that it was not the institution of the Jim Crow School that has deprived this nation of the black scientist who might have solved the technological kinks delaying our satellite launching?"

For Christine Mann, reading the news brought mixed emotions. She felt fear, certainly. She had been just three years old when the first atomic bombs were dropped on Japan. She was part of the first generation in the history of the world to grow up with the possibility of the human race becoming extinct due to nuclear war.

The hostility between the United States and the Soviet Union made the country anxious about nuclear war. Black-and-yellow triangular fallout shelter signs popped up in public spaces, pointing the way to underground bomb shelters that were supposed to provide protection in the event of a nuclear attack. At school, students practiced "duck-and-cover" drills under their desks.

At the same time, Christine felt a sense of wonder, even a thrill, to see a satellite circling Earth in the skies above. The world beyond Earth had always been a mysterious place. Space travel was becoming a natural next step for the restless inhabitants of Earth, not just the subject of science fiction. What had been a dream was becoming reality.

Christine and many other Americans worried that the Soviets had traveled into space before the Americans. *We can't let them beat us,* she thought, echoing the sentiments shared by those who worked at the Langley Laboratory and citizens across America.

Black-and-yellow fallout shelter signs were used to identify shelters in case of nuclear or chemical warfare during the Cold War. **Federal Highway Administration — MUTCD.**

A New Day

Three years before Christine Mann's parents had enrolled her at the Allen School, she had attended a public school in Monroe, North Carolina. She remembered the day in 1954 when the principal stepped into her eighth-grade classroom and made an an-

147

nouncement: "I just came to let you all know that the Supreme Court just ruled on *Brown v. Board of Education,* and you will be going to school with white students in the future." The judges in the five legal cases known together as *Brown v. Board of Education* ruled that it was illegal to separate black and white students in public schools.

In fact, the *Brown v. Board of Education* court cases had a special connection for Dorothy Vaughan. A sixteen-year-old girl named Barbara Johns, a student at Moton High School in Farmville, where Dorothy had taught, had grown tired of Moton's overcrowded classrooms and tattered textbooks. When one of the school's broken-down school buses crashed, killing five of her classmates, Barbara decided to take action. She led her fellow students in a strike, refusing to go to school until authorities improved the black school's conditions; Dorothy Vaughan's relatives were among the participants. Barbara then contacted lawyers, who helped the students file a lawsuit against the county school board. It took years, but the lawsuit filed by Barbara Johns and her classmates eventually made its way to the Supreme Court, where it became part of the *Brown* decision.

It was a victory for those who wanted to

abolish segregation in America's public schools. But it would also mean a big change for both whites and blacks. Christine and her classmates were shocked when the principal made the announcement. She lived in the segregated part of a small Southern town, where all of her neighbors were black — the doctors, the teachers, the street sweepers, everyone. Most of the black men in her part of town earned a living working for the railroad. Black women worked in the cotton mill or as housekeepers. Segregation was all that Christine had ever known, so she worried about the *Brown* decision. She feared that she and her classmates would not be good enough or smart enough to succeed in a classroom of white children. How could she and other African American students, coming from overcrowded classrooms with old textbooks, compete with the kids who lived in the white section of town, across the railroad tracks?

But Christine's parents — just like Dorothy Vaughan's, Katherine Goble's, and Mary Jackson's — would do anything they could to help their daughter succeed. They believed in "education, honesty, hard work, and character." Christine's father earned a good living as an insurance salesman. Hers was one of the few black families in town that owned a car, a Pontiac Hydramatic. And Christine's time at the Allen School was providing her with the best possible start in life.

A charismatic eleventh-grade geometry teacher sparked Christine's interest in math, and she began to consider a future that would use her skills as a mathematician. Christine followed in the family tradition of attending a black college; she chose Hampton Institute. The summer before her senior year, Christine had accompanied a friend to the friend's sister's graduation from the school, and she had fallen in love with the elegant campus and balmy breezes from the ocean. She applied to Hampton and received a scholarship from the United Negro College Fund.

Christine graduated from the Allen School in May 1958. From the time *Sputnik* took flight in October 1957 until she addressed her classmates as valedictorian in the spring, the Soviets had launched two more satellites, *Sputnik 2* and *Sputnik 3*. In August 1958, Christine left North Carolina and with her family drove north to the Hampton Institute campus. She didn't know it at the time, but her decision to move to Hampton would make her a part of the tradition of

150

women working as mathematicians at Langley.

The mountains of North Carolina flattened out as Christine's family drove toward the coast. She always loved the mountains, but when she saw the James River — so broad and measured in its flow as it joined Chesapeake Bay — the sight took her breath away. Crossing that river as she closed in on Hampton, Virginia, made Christine feel like anything was possible.

16

WHAT A DIFFERENCE
A DAY MAKES

Christine Mann wasn't the only person who spent her evenings staring up at the sky. Katherine Goble stood outside on a warm October night in 1957 and watched the winking dot of light in the sky as it moved low across the horizon. At Langley Memorial Aeronautics Laboratory in Hampton, Virginia, and across the country, Americans turned their eyes skyward with a mixture of wonder and terror. As they tried to see *Sputnik* from their backyards they asked themselves: Could the 183-pound metal sphere launched into orbit by the Russians see them, too? It became a game as they surfed the radio dial trying to lock onto the sound of the satellite beeping, a sound like that of an otherworldly cricket. This was *Sputnik*.

In the 1940s, designing aircraft capable of flying beyond Earth's atmosphere had seemed too far-fetched. Now, with *Sputnik* circling overhead every ninety-six minutes, Americans wanted to know how the United States had fallen behind.

The stakes were high, or it seemed that way at the time. "First in space means first, period," said Senate Majority Leader Lyndon B. Johnson. "Second in space is second in everything."

The Challenge of Space

Katherine Goble had wondered what the next challenge would be for Langley researchers, and *Sputnik* gave her the answer.

Space had long been a "dirty word" at airplane-focused Langley, something that the researchers weren't really supposed to spend their time working on. Congress had warned the researchers not to waste taxpayer money on "science fiction" and dreams of manned spaceflight. The laboratory was tasked with designing and improving aircraft that had practical applications right here on Earth.

That didn't stop Langley engineers from imagining how missile shapes and rocket engines and solutions to reentry problems involved in high-speed flight research might apply to space vehicles. Any aircraft that traveled into space first had to pass through the layers of Earth's atmosphere, accelerating through the sound barrier and then escaping the pull of Earth's gravity before settling into the 18,000-miles-per-hour speed that characterized objects locked into low Earth orbit. On the return trip, the same vehicle would have to skid through the friction of the increasingly dense atmosphere, encountering heat that could reach 3,000 degrees Fahrenheit before falling back to Earth.

Now that the Russians had a head start in space, the United States was eager to join the race, but engineers debated about how to start. Some favored an aircraft designed like a plane that could elegantly orbit Earth and then glide back through the atmosphere. But that might take too much time. With beating the Russians now a national priority, engineers felt pressure to find the quickest, surest way into space.

The Flight Research Division, where Katherine Goble worked, specialized in doing research involving real planes, not parts or models, like people who worked in the wind tunnels. Another group at Langley, the Pilotless Aircraft Research Division (PARD), specialized in rockets and had set

An aerial view of the launch pad at Wallops Flight Facility on Wallops Island, Virginia. National Aeronautics and Space Administration.

up a test range on Wallops Island off the Virginia coast where test rockets could be launched. In previous tests, the group's rockets had reached speeds of Mach 15 in flight, and the engineers in PARD were confident that their vehicles were powerful enough to lift a satellite and human passenger into orbit. The engineers in the Flight Research Division and in PARD were eager to test their ideas about how to catch up to the Russians in space.

From the NACA to NASA

A number of agencies wanted to manage the space program. The US Air Force, the US Naval Research Observatory, and the Army Ballistic Missile Agency bid for the assignment, but the National Advisory Committee for Aeronautics, where Katherine, Mary, Dorothy, and the other female computers worked, was chosen to lead the efforts. It was an exciting time for them all. Hampton, Virginia, was going to be the center of the space program! In October 1958, the US government combined all of the various space-related groups. The expanded agency had a new name: the National Aeronautics and Space Administration, or NASA.

The NACA had become NASA, but the change meant more than just a different name. While the NACA had been quiet, obscure, and largely unnoticed, NASA would be very high-profile and high-stakes, and scrutinized by the world. And the women working here would have higher-profile jobs, too. The work done by the NACA engineers had been hidden behind the more public operations of the military and commercial aircraft manufacturers. NASA was tasked to "provide for the widest practicable and appropriate dissemination of information concerning its activities." That meant the work done at NASA belonged to every American. All of its actions — its moments of triumph and its heartbreaking failures and tragedies — were to be laid bare to the citizens and broadcast on television.

Katherine Goble also wanted to beat the Russians. She didn't want the *Sputnik* challenge to go unanswered. In addition to national pride, she personally longed to do something untried, untested, and unexplored. Katherine wanted to be part of the team that would figure out how to send humans into space.

The End of West Computing

As the National Aeronautics and Space Act of 1958, which called for the creation of NASA, made its way through Congress, another memo quietly circulated through the Langley Research Center, the former Langley Memorial Aeronautical Laboratory. "The West Area Computing Unit is dissolved." Slowly but surely, women from West Computing, like their white counterparts, had begun to receive permanent assignments in different engineering groups. Now, only nine women remained in Dorothy's pool.

Dorothy Vaughan had seen this day coming since the East Computing pool was disbanded in 1947. Each new facility in the laboratory fueled the demand for specialization among its professionals, including the mathematicians. The idea of operating a central computing pool had become obsolete.

The computing pool had created rare opportunities for women at the NACA. Getting hired by the laboratory as a professional mathematician had been an important and ground-breaking step for women, especially the African-American women. But now, the times were changing. Aeronautical research had become more complex, and the laboratory needed mathematicians with specialized knowledge. Women like Dorothy Hoover, Katherine Goble, and Mary Jackson had gotten their start in West Computing and moved on. Now it was time for the pool itself, and its leader, to move on, too. The days of the West Computing office had come to an end.

The end of West Area Computing was bittersweet to Dorothy Vaughan. On the one hand, it meant the end of segregation at Langley. Now, the black women would work with white engineers and white computers, instead of having to stay in their own office.

Dorothy had worked hard to support the careers of women like Katherine Goble and Mary Jackson, and give West Computing a reputation for doing work that was as good as that of their white colleagues. The end of West Computing was, in many ways, a long-fought-for victory. The standards upheld by the women of West Computing created opportunities for a new generation of women with passion for math and hopes for a career beyond teaching.

On the other hand, it meant the end of Dorothy's career as a manager. It had taken her eight years to reach her seat at the front of the West Computing office. For seven years after that she ruled a room full of black female mathematicians doing research at the world's most prestigious aeronautical laboratory. But now, she, too, was being moved to another group, with a new boss.

Dorothy was forty-eight years old in October 1958. Her older children were now entering college. She was proud of the way she had navigated through the days of racial segregation, proud of whatever small share she might claim in fighting prejudice with intellectual merit. During her years at West Computing, Dorothy had watched scores of women move from the computing pool to other positions within the laboratory. She and the other female computers had proven that given the opportunity and support, women were just as smart as men.

Dorothy had never been one to linger over the past. For better or worse, Langley's fresh start was giving Dorothy Vaughan a fresh start as well.

17

WRITING THE
TEXTBOOK ON SPACE

The staff at the Langley Research Center had very few resources to teach engineers about outer space. To bring the entire laboratory up to speed, Katherine Goble's branch chief organized a lecture series to take place from February to May 1958. He asked his team, the engineers in the Flight Research and the Pilotless Aircraft Research Divisions, to present the lectures on a range of topics, from the solar system to problems with reentry from outer space into Earth's atmosphere. The lectures were a crash course in all things aeronautic.

Katherine Goble loved learning everything she could about space travel. She was delighted when the engineers in her group assigned her the task of preparing charts for use in these space technology lectures. In essence, she was helping the engineers write the first real textbook about outer space.

Always curious, Katherine listened to everything her coworkers said. She read every word of *Aviation Week,* a magazine about flight. She drained every drop of knowledge from the engineers she worked with, but that was not enough. The real action, she knew, was taking place in the lectures and editorial meetings, those private closed-door gatherings where engineers reviewed and discussed the most recent research reports. She wanted to be part of those talks, but the men in charge would not allow it.

A Place at the Table

Building an airplane was nothing compared to getting research through Langley's grueling literature review process. "Present your case, build it, sell it so they believe it" — that was the Langley way. Authors of a NASA technical report had to talk about their research and give a lot of information to convince everyone that their theory was correct. Then they faced questions from four or five people chosen for their expertise in a topic. Sometimes these questions were really tough. The committee members looked for inaccuracies, inconsistencies, incomprehensible statements, and illogical conclusions in the report. After clearing the technical hurdles, a report went through a style, clarity, and grammatical check. A final report might take months or even years to complete.

Katherine Goble sat down with the engineers to review the requirements for the space technology lectures and the research reports that were coming out of the presentations. She asked lots of questions so that she completely understood the problems set before her.

"Why can't I go to the editorial meetings?" she asked the engineers.

"Girls don't go to the meetings," her colleagues said.

"Is there a law against it?" she asked.

There wasn't, of course. It wasn't personal, the engineers told her. It was just the way things had always been done. The no-woman rule was a matter of practice, not policy. Langley gave each division chief and branch head the power to manage their own groups. These male bosses decided whether a woman was promoted, if she got a raise, or if she was permitted to attend meetings.

Women at Langley had to learn how to work with men. They needed to be polite, but not so polite that they seemed timid.

For the most part, men were engineers and women were computers. Men did the analytical thinking and women did the calculations. Men gave the orders and women took the notes. Unless an engineer was given a compelling reason to see a woman as a peer, she remained in his blind spot. Even the smartest woman might get stuck doing repetitive, humdrum work unless someone paid attention and gave her a chance.

Women like Katherine Goble found their work interesting, just like the men did. For the women who found their true calling at NASA, they matched their male colleagues in curiosity, passion, and the ability to withstand pressure. The problem was that women had to get over the high hurdle of low expectations — they needed to prove that they were just as good as men and should be held to the same standards and given the same opportunities.

Whatever personal insecurities Katherine Goble may have had about being a woman working with men or about being one of the few blacks in a white workplace, she didn't let them bother her. Male or female, black or white, as far as Katherine was concerned, once she got to the office, "they were all the same."

"Why can't I go to the editorial meetings?" Katherine Goble asked again. On this issue, like any other, she kept up the questioning until she received a satisfactory answer. Her requests came across as gentle but persistent. She wasn't going to let the issue drop. The greatest adventure in the history of humankind was happening in the office next door, and she wanted to be part of it.

"Let her go," one of the men finally said, exasperated. The others agreed, no doubt tired of saying no. Who were they, they must have figured, to stand in the way of someone so committed to making a contribution?

In 1958, Katherine Goble finally made it into the editorial meetings of the Guidance and Control Branch of Langley's Flight Research Division, soon to be renamed the Aerospace Mechanics Division of NASA. She took her place at the table, where she knew she belonged. She had a lot to learn and a lot to offer.

18

WITH ALL DELIBERATE SPEED

In 1958, Katherine Goble and her research group took on what seemed like the world's most interesting challenge: sending a human being into space. NASA reorganized the research teams so that they were doing all they could do turn spaceflight from a comic book fantasy into a reality. The Space Task Group, set up to be the nerve center of the new operation, was made up of many engineers and female computers from Katherine's group, the Flight Research Division, and PARD, the rocket specialists. The new group decided that their first space mission needed an appropriate name, so they decided to call the effort Project Mercury, named for the god of travelers in Roman mythology.

The space program brought a lot of attention to Hampton, Virginia. Unfortunately, even as the engineers and mathematicians at Langley embraced the future, the state seemed stuck in the past, unwilling to let go of its segregationist policies. Virginia's legacy as the birthplace of humanity's first step into the heavens would have to compete with its embarrassing reputation as the country's most outspoken opponent to the integration of public schools.

Virginia schools were in chaos. Some schools had tried to comply with the Supreme Court's decision requiring states to integrate their schools "with all deliberate speed." The governor refused to allow integration, so he ordered that the doors to those schools be chained shut. Thirteen thousand students found themselves sitting at home in the fall of 1958.

Black and white families struggled to send their children to private schools or to move their school-age children to live with relatives in other areas where they could get an education. In 1959, Virginia's government finally reopened most of the schools in the state. But the administrators in Prince Edward County — which included Farmville, and Dorothy Vaughan's former high school, R. R. Moton — chose to defund the school system rather than integrate; they just stopped giving the schools the money they needed to stay open. The Prince Edward schools remained closed from 1959 through 1964.

In other parts of the state, including those in the Hampton Roads area, the schools remained open but segregated. Despite the *Brown v. Board of Education* decision making segregation illegal, in the fall of 1958, the children of Langley's black and white employees returned to their separate routines at their separate schools.

Katherine Goble didn't have energy to spend fighting with the local school system. She didn't approve of segregation, but she wanted her children to get a good education. She continued to push her children to excel in their segregated schools.

She was still trying to balance the demands of being a single mother and working at a demanding job. She still lived with the grief of having lost her husband years before, but she didn't let that side of her life show in public. Between work life and home life, Katherine regularly attended worship services and sang in the church choir.

One evening in 1958, a handsome thirty-three-year-old army captain named James Johnson came to choir practice at Katherine's church. He had grown up in Hampton and trained in aviation metal-smithing. During World War II, he became an expert in aircraft maintenance and repair. After completing his service, he landed a clerk job at the Commerce Department in Washington, DC. He also signed up for the US Navy Reserve, repairing planes for test flights. He loved planes just as much as Katherine did.

Katherine hadn't intended to fall in love, but she and James — Jim — began dating. Jim's devotion to the military made it easy for him to understand Katherine's commitment to her work at Langley. He was also sensitive to the secretive nature of her work and the long hours it demanded. During this intense period of competition with the Russians, people at Langley often worked until 10:00 p.m. or later.

The Mercury Mission

Katherine worked long hours on her new assignment involving Project Mercury. In a less urgent time, the researchers at NASA might have followed a slower and more systematic approach to their work, conducting careful and measured investigations of all possible options in space travel. With the Russians off to what looked like a commanding lead, NASA sought the simplest, fastest, and most reliable way to get into space.

The engineers approached Project Mercury by breaking it down into its constituent parts. One team looked at the shape of the aircraft, determining that it should be streamlined to minimize aerodynamic drag. Another team of researchers showed that a needle-shaped structure would most efficiently deflect the extreme heat caused when the aircraft zoomed through the atmosphere on reentry. They recommended a blunt-based body — something shaped like a cork — which would create a shock wave as it came back to Earth, minimizing the extreme heat and keeping the person inside safe.

The spacecraft would have to be small, so astronauts could be no taller than five feet, eleven inches and had to weigh less than 180 pounds. Each astronaut candidate was required to be a qualified test pilot younger than forty years old with at least a bachelor's degree. After months of searching, NASA selected the final crew. In 1959, NASA held a press conference to present the "Mercury Seven" astronauts to the world: Alan Shepard, Gus Grissom, Gordon Cooper, Wally Schirra, Deke Slayton, John Glenn, and Scott Carpenter.

There was a great deal of preparation to be done by everyone — from researcher to astronaut — before takeoff of the spacecraft. NASA assigned the astronauts to an office on the Langley campus next door to the Space Task Group. Langley employees loved catching a glimpse of the astronauts, who had become celebrities, walking around the campus. The Mercury Seven trained hard, both physically and in the classroom, preparing their bodies and minds for the unprecedented journey ahead of them.

While the astronauts were preparing for this important mission, Katherine Goble had to calculate the flight trajectories. In other words, she had to plan the exact path that the spacecraft would travel across Earth's surface, from the moment it lifted off the launch pad and flew through the atmosphere and into space, until it splashed back down in the Atlantic Ocean. Project Mercury required so much work that the Space Task Group, which coordinated all aspects of the space mission, relied on other divisions at Langley and at other NASA centers to help carry out their gargantuan task. Day after day, the team pored over equations, scrawled ideas on blackboards, evaluated each other's work, erased it, started over.

Katherine's new job, trajectory analysis, involved the study of how a projectile moved through space, both here on Earth and in outer space. This work was similar to that done by other female computers who spent thousands upon thousands of woman-hours computing mathematical tables, which soldiers used to figure out how to fire their weapons and hit their targets.

The Space Task Group decided that the best way to send the first person into space was with a simple ballistic flight. The capsule would be fired into space like a bullet from a gun or a tennis ball from a ball machine. The first spacecraft would not have any propulsion of its own. The capsule would go up, then come down and land in the Atlantic Ocean. Where the capsule landed depended on where it was launched. The calculations had to be exact so that the astronaut would return close enough to waiting US Navy ships to be quickly hoisted out of the water and pulled to safety.

Katherine understood that carrying out an orbital mission would be more difficult than the simpler ballistic flights. The team would have to plan the journey so precisely that the spacecraft would pass through the atmosphere, hurtle along on a looping circle around the planet, and land in exactly the right place.

"Let me do it," Katherine said to her boss. Working as a computer (or "math aide," as the women were now called under NASA), Katherine had proven herself. She was older than many of the engineers she worked with, but she matched them at every turn for intelligence, enthusiasm, and work stamina. "Tell me where you want the man to land, and I'll tell you where to send him up."

Katherine knew the math as well as anyone else on the team. An engineer named Ted Skopinski was assigned the task of preparing the research report, and as his computer, Katherine assisted him. He thought she was smart and he respected her work, so he gave her the opportunity to take on challenging assignments. She had to consider factors that were unique to an orbital flight. For example, she needed to take into account the fact that Earth isn't a perfect sphere, but a little bit squat, like a mandarin orange. She also had to factor in the speed of Earth's rotation. Everything had to be spelled out, quantified, and identified.

Over the months of 1959, a thirty-four-page research paper began to take shape. It was remarkably complex, filled with equations, charts, and tables of calculations.

"Katherine should finish the report," said Ted, the engineer she had been collaborating with. "She's done most of the work anyway."

Katherine's boss Henry had a reputation for being less than supportive of the advancement of female employees, but Ted encouraged her to put the finishing touches on her report. Her boss grudgingly gave in after Ted made the case for her. The report was titled "Determination of Azimuth Angle at Burnout for Placing a Satellite Over a Selected Earth Position." After ten months of editorial meetings, analysis, recommendations, and revisions, the report was published in September 1960. It was the first time a woman working in the Aerospace Mechanics Division had managed to get her name on a research report.

For Katherine, the completion of the report marked the beginning of a new phase of her life, not just at Langley but at home, too. Somehow, during the long days of 1959, she accepted an offer even more enticing than being invited to the editorial meetings at work: Jim Johnson asked her to marry him. The coupled wed in August 1959. When she put her name on the final draft of her first research report, she signed her new name: Katherine G. Johnson.

19

MODEL BEHAVIOR

While Katherine Johnson busied herself with the equations that would determine the path that the first Americans would follow into outer space, Mary Jackson focused on making supersonic airplanes even faster and more efficient. Mary loved her job at Langley, but she also loved using her technical skills in other ways. One summer, she had a special project in mind: rather than devote her talents to improving a high-speed aircraft that burned through the skies, Mary decided to lend her trained eye and her understanding of aerodynamics to help her son, Levi, build a car to enter the Virginia Peninsula's 1960 soap box derby.

Mary and Levi had gone to the local Chevrolet dealer to fill out the entry form and pick up a copy of the official rules. "The car and driver together must weigh less than 250 pounds. Only rubber wheels allowed. Length shall not exceed 80 inches. Road clearance must be at least three inches with the driver in the car. The total cost of the car shall not exceed $10.00, exclusive of wheels and axles."

Since the beginning of the year, Mary had spent hundreds of hours working with her thirteen-year-old son on the motorless car. They had made sketches and measurements, testing different designs until they settled on one. They searched the clutter in the back of the garage for things that could be useful: vegetable crates, plywood, wagon wheels, garden tools, old shoes, wire and twine — almost anything could be put into service. The race, held over the Fourth of July weekend, was fast approaching.

On race day, Levi and the other competitors started at the peak of the Twenty-Fifth Street Bridge in Newport News, the only hill in the flat-as-a-pancake coastal area. At the signal to go, the drivers released their brakes and hunched down into the cockpits of their vehicles, waiting for gravity to take them down the nine-hundred-foot racecourse.

The All-American Soap Box Derby mixed American ingenuity with family fun. (At

A group of boys waiting their turn to participate in a soap box derby, competing to see whose homemade vehicles went fastest. **Bibliothèque et Archives nationales du Quebec.**

least for boys, since girls weren't allowed to compete in the race until the early 1970s.) The competition started as a Depression-era activity, a way to create fun and excitement at a time when they were difficult to come by. By 1960, more than fifty thousand boys competed in races around the country.

The competition was popular in the Hampton area. Officially the derby was the boys' show. Parents were supposed to sit back and only offer advice, but many parents enjoyed the engineering project at least as much as their children did. Many NASA engineers hoped their children would some-day choose to follow in their professional footsteps. They wouldn't get rich, but an engineer's salary was more than enough to enjoy a comfortable, middle-class lifestyle.

When it came to the derby, no NASA father had anything on Mary Jackson. She treated the soap box derby car as an ap-prenticeship in engineering. It didn't stop there. At school, she pushed Levi to take the most challenging math and science classes he could handle, and she coached him on his science projects.

Many African-American boys didn't know about the All-American Soap Box Derby, or they didn't think it was for them. Starting early in the year, Chevrolet placed ads in *Boys' Life* magazine, the official publication of the Boy Scouts. Some African Americans read the ad, but they frequently disqualified themselves from participating in competi-tions even without the "Whites Only" sign: there was no rule keeping black boys from entering the race, but it took a lot of cour-age, and a mind that saw the experience as something open to all boys regardless of their color, for them to give it a try.

The Race

On Saturday, July 3, a crowd of four thousand people gathered along both sides of the Twenty-Fifth Street Bridge. It was a clear, warm day, with just enough breeze to keep the spectators from getting hot.

Contestants for the first heat wheeled their cars to the starting line and settled in the cockpits. Officials weighed and inspected each car, then held a lottery to determine the positions in the first heat. At the crack of the starter's pistol, the pint-sized pilots released their brakes and rolled down the hill.

The race was an all-day event. Mary Jackson could almost see the air moving around the cars just as clearly as if she were analyzing data from a wind tunnel. Her son's car was well made; the only adjustment it needed was "a drop of oil on each wheel bearing."

Levi won one heat after another. Then he got into position for the final competition. By the time he reached the finish line, Mary was shouting with delight: Levi won! Wearing a black-and-white crash helmet and the official race T-shirt, Levi had sailed across the finish line at a blazing 17 miles per hour.

When interviewed about his victory by the newspapers, Levi explained that the secret to his victory was the slimness of his machine, which helped to lower the wind resistance.

Levi won a gold trophy, a new bicycle, and a spot at the national All-American Soap Box Derby in Akron, Ohio. There he would face off against drivers from around the country in front of seventy-five thousand fans on a track where speeds could exceed thirty miles per hour.

Levi Jackson was the "first colored boy in history" to win the Hampton Roads area's soap box derby. From the moment he won, donations started rolling in from black community service organizations and social clubs, black-owned businesses, and black churches, all eager to support Levi's big trip to Akron. The African-American community shared Levi's victory. If a black kid could take home the soap box derby trophy, what else might be possible?

Achievement through hard work, social progress through science — that's what Mary believed in. When Levi took the first-place trophy, she was bursting with pride. When a reporter for the *Norfolk Journal and Guide* asked Levi what he wanted to do when he grew up, he said, "I want to be an engineer like my mother."

Being a "Black First" — the first black

person to have achieved a particular goal —
was a powerful symbol, Mary Jackson knew
just as well as anyone. She embraced her
son's achievement with delight, but she also
knew that the best thing about breaking a
barrier was that it would never have to be
broken again.

Possibilities for Women

Mary Jackson believed that achievement
worked like a bank account. It was something you drew on when you were in need
and made deposits to when you had a
surplus. Girls, she believed, needed particular support: it wasn't lost on Mary that the
derby, while open to her son, would have
rejected her daughter's application.

At work, she and the other female mathematicians were no strangers to encountering barriers based on their gender. Despite
the relatively large number of women now
working at NASA, most female technical
professionals — black and white — were
classified as mathematicians or computers,
rather than engineers. They were paid less,
even if they were doing the same work.

Mary developed allies among the white
women she worked with. She asked one
white colleague to participate in a career
panel in 1962, organized by the local chap-

ter of the National Council of Negro Women. The woman agreed, and they presented a joint lecture, "The Aspects of Engineering for Women," at an all-black junior high school. Their appearance on the stage together made a powerful statement about the possibilities of the engineering field for black girls. Mary was black, and her colleague Emma Jean was white; Mary was short, and Emma Jean was tall. They looked different but they worked with each other, and they also worked with men.

Mary had earned her engineering title through hard work, talent, and drive, but she knew she owed a debt of gratitude to those women who had led the way. Each woman who had come before had cracked the hole in the wall a little wider, allowing the next talent to come through. Now Mary wanted to make room for the women coming behind her.

20

DEGREES OF FREEDOM

In February 1960, as the Space Task Group pushed forward with tests of the Mercury capsule, four students from North Carolina Agricultural and Technical, a black college in Greensboro, North Carolina, sat down in the whites-only section of the lunch counter at a Woolworth's drugstore. David Richmond, Franklin McCain, Ezell Blair, Jr., and Joseph McNeil tried to order a cup of coffee. The staff refused to serve them. The manager asked them to leave, but the students refused to leave until the store closed later that night.

That nonviolent protest was just the beginning of what would become a new phase of the civil rights movement. The following day, the "Greensboro Four" had turned into twenty activists. On the third day, sixty students gathered at the Woolworth's, and on the fourth day, three hundred had joined the demonstration.

Within a week, similar peaceful protests had spread to other cities in North Carolina and then into Kentucky, Tennessee, and Virginia. The students called their protests "sit-downs" or "sit-ins." Sometimes, the police arrested the protesters and took them off to jail. The prison sentences that followed didn't discourage the activists. They did not intend to back down until they had defeated segregation.

Protests in Hampton

Hampton Institute in Virginia — the school from which Mary Jackson graduated — was the first school outside of North Carolina to organize a sit-in. The college had a direct link to the civil rights movement. Five years before, Rosa Parks, a seamstress in Montgomery, Alabama, had refused to give her seat on a city bus to a white man, triggering a bus boycott led by Martin Luther King Jr. Parks received death threats, and she and her husband were fired from their jobs in Alabama. The president of Hampton Institute offered Parks a job working as a hostess at the university's faculty dining room. She accepted, and she worked there from

1957 to 1958.

When the sit-ins came to Hampton years later, Christine Mann, who had left her home in North Carolina behind to attend college in Virginia, was an eighteen-year-old junior. She wanted to pursue a career in the sciences, but her father insisted that she also earn a teaching certificate as a backup plan in case she had trouble finding work. In addition to taking courses in math and physics, Christine became involved in the civil rights movement.

In protests that resembled those in Greensboro, Christine and some of her classmates marched to the lunch counter at the local drugstore in downtown Hampton. They tried to order food, but the attendants at the counter refused to serve them, so they then sat, reading or working on homework assignments. They were quietly protesting. When they refused to leave, the owner shut down the store in the middle of the afternoon. The next month, five hundred students staged a peaceful protest in downtown Hampton.

"We want to be treated as American citizens," said the outspoken leaders of the student movement. "If this means integration in all areas of life, then that is what we want."

The Hampton Institute campus was alive with the possibility of significant social change. Christine also joined voter registration drives, walking door-to-door in black neighborhoods urging residents to register to vote in the November 1960 elections.

A rumor circulated on campus that the astronauts supported the student protests. The astronauts represented mainstream America. The very idea that those buzz-cut, middle American men were standing with the student activists, adding their voices to the call for equal opportunity for all Americans, was thrilling. It didn't matter if it was true. It inspired them either way.

Progress at Langley in the 1960s

The culture was changing at the Langley Research Center, too. When Dorothy Vaughan turned off the lights in the West Area Computing office for the last time, she and the remaining women in the segregated pool were sent out to other divisions at the lab. The era of West Computing — a separate division for African-American women — was over.

Dorothy Vaughan was assigned to the newly built computer complex on Langley's west side. By the 1960s, Langley had centralized its computing operations into a group named the Analysis and Computation Division. It served all of the center's research operations as well as providing electronic computing services to outside contractors. In the new division, Dorothy was reunited with many of the West Computers, as well as with other women who had worked in East Computing.

More striking than the racial integration of the female mathematicians was the fact that men had joined the team. Computing had been promoted in status from being an all-female service organization to a respected coed division. Computing was no longer considered women's work.

However, with the increasing use of computer technology in aeronautical research, some of the older women at Langley, who still did most of their work using the older-model mechanical calculators, fell out of touch. The early 1960s were a time of change in the history of computing, a dividing line between the time when computers were human and when they were machines. Computing jobs were no longer handed off to a roomful of women punching numbers into $500 mechanical calculating machines; room-sized computers that cost more than $1 million each now did the same work — and did it many times faster.

Faced with this new era in computing, fifty-year-old Dorothy Vaughan reinvented herself as a computer programmer. Engineers still came to her and asked for help. Now, instead of assigning the task to one of her staff or doing the computations herself, she programmed the calculations into an IBM computer and let the machine do the math.

In the past, Dorothy would have set up the equations in a data sheet and showed one of the women computers how to fill it out. As a computer programmer, she converted the equations into the computer's language, FORTRAN, by using a special machine to punch holes into 7 3/8–by–1 3/4-inch cards. Each card represented one set of instructions for the computer.

The longer or more complex the program, the more cards Dorothy or another programmer fed into the computer. The machines could not take more than two thousand cards, or two thousand lines of instructions. Even modest programs could require a tray with hundreds of cards, which had to remain in the correct order.

As powerful as the computers were, Project Mercury required even more electronic brainpower than Langley had available. At the end of 1960, NASA purchased two IBM

Dorothy Vaughan (left) with other female computers at a social event in the 1960s. NASA-Langley.

7090 computers and installed them in a state-of-the-art facility in Washington, DC. That computer lab was part of the Goddard Space Flight Center, which opened in 1959 in Greenbelt, Maryland. NASA established a third computer data center in Bermuda. Together these three computers would be able to monitor and analyze all aspects of the space flights, from launch to splashdown.

Keeping in Touch

Orbiting Earth presented a number of communication challenges for NASA engineers. It was one thing to have a flight take off from Cape Canaveral, Florida, and land in the Atlantic Ocean. These flights stayed within the communication range of Mission Control in Florida and the data centers in DC and Bermuda.

Orbital flights — missions that sent an astronaut around the globe — were much more dangerous. The aircraft would pass out of visual and radio contact with Mission Control for extended periods of time. NASA demanded constant contact with the astronaut every minute of every orbit.

The engineers at Langley had to build a worldwide communication network between Mission Control and the orbiting spacecraft. Developing the two-way communication and tracking network was almost as challenging as building the spacecraft itself. It required the creation of eighteen communications stations set up around the globe so that the orbiting astronaut was never out of touch.

The computers also sounded the alarm at the first sign of trouble. Any deviation from the projected flight path, evidence of malfunction on board the capsule, or abnormal vital signs from the astronaut would send Mission Control scrambling to solve the problem.

Engineers at Langley struggled to make their deadlines, but they couldn't afford to make any mistakes. The projected launch date slipped from 1960 to 1961.

During this period, the Soviets struck again. On April 12, 1961, Russian cosmonaut Yuri Gagarin became the first human in space and the first human to orbit Earth.

"We could have beaten them, we should have beaten them," Project Mercury's flight director, the engineer in charge of coordinating many of the aspects of the mission, said years later.

NASA engineers didn't feel defeated and they didn't experience the panic that followed the launch of *Sputnik.* The Soviet success was frustrating and embarrassing, but the Langley team responded with renewed passion for their mission. NASA and its network of contractors focused their talents and kept working. They were almost ready to launch.

The Mercury Mission

It would take a total of 1.2 million tests, simulations, investigations, inspections, verifications, experiments, checkouts, and dry runs to send the first American into space. It also took several failed rocket tests and a hair-raising suborbital flight with a chimpanzee on board; the capsule landed so far from the recovery ships that it was nearly underwater when it was finally plucked from the ocean. "Ham" the Astrochimp survived the flight. (His name is an acronym for the lab that prepped him for his mission, the Holloman Aerospace Medical Center.)

In a courageous move, NASA decided to broadcast the launch of *Mercury-Redstone 3* live on television. This would be the third time the *Redstone* rocket would be used to boost the Mercury capsule into flight over the Atlantic Ocean. At least forty-five million Americans tuned in to watch the success — or failure — of the first United States manned space mission.

Astronaut Alan Shepard strapped into the capsule, just six feet in diameter and less than seven feet high. The launch was successful and the spacecraft soared to an altitude of 116.5 miles above the earth.

The suborbital flight of the capsule Shepard named *Freedom 7* lasted only fifteen minutes and twenty-two seconds and covered 303 miles. Freedom 7 was a pale technological achievement compared to the

Russian cosmonaut's flight the month before, but its success helped President John F. Kennedy make a promise to the country to complete a goal significantly more ambitious: a manned mission to the moon.

"I believe that this nation should commit itself to achieving the goal, before this decade is out, of landing a man on the moon and returning him safely to Earth," President Kennedy said before a session of Congress, three weeks after Shepard splashed down.

Every NASA employee involved with the space program started to worry. They were already working nights and weekends to prepare for six more scheduled Mercury flights. NASA still hadn't completed its first orbital flight, and President Kennedy had promised they were going to send a man to the moon. Was that an impossible dream?

It was a terrifying prospect and the most exhilarating thing they had ever heard. Getting to the moon — one of mankind's deepest and most enduring fantasies — had long been the private dream of many at Langley as well. But with only one operational success under its belt and with six Mercury missions to go, NASA's road to the moon seemed unimaginably complex. The engi-

The mission to the moon was a pledge made by John F. Kennedy, thirty-fifth president of the United States. JFK Library.

neers estimated that the upcoming orbital flight, including the fully manned global tracking network, required a team of eighteen thousand people. It would take many times more than that to complete a lunar landing.

A New Mission Control
It became clear that NASA was going to have to expand its facilities and workforce if

the program was going to reach the goal of putting a man on the moon. And then rumors spread that the Space Task Group was going to be leaving Hampton, Virginia. The Langley employees campaigned to keep Mission Control at their base, but NASA was considering other sites. In 1960, nine locations were shortlisted as possibilities, but Virginia was not one of them. Powerful Texans in Congress used their influence, and Houston was chosen as the site.

With Project Mercury in full swing and a brand-new research center ready to open in Houston — NASA named it the Manned Spacecraft Center — the space program had more work than it could handle. Katherine Johnson had been asked to transfer to Houston with the group, but she and her husband decided to remain in Virginia in order to stay close to their families.

Mission Control might have moved to Houston, but Langley was still a beehive of space activity for Katherine Johnson and her colleagues, who were busy laying the groundwork for meeting NASA's greatest challenge, sending a man to the moon and bringing him safely home.

21

OUT OF THE PAST, THE FUTURE

Sending a man into space was a tall order, but it was the part about returning him safely to Earth that kept Katherine Johnson and the rest of the Langley employees awake at night. There were countless ways that things could go wrong, and they needed to be ready for each one.

The rocket had to operate flawlessly. The Atlas rocket was going to be used to take the Mercury capsule into orbit, but it was temperamental. Two of its five previous launches had ended in failure. One rocket had surged into the sky, then exploded mid-air.

There seemed to be an infinite number of things that could go wrong with the space-craft. The space capsule itself was a sophisticated tin can, but one that required elaborate engineering. The vehicle's oxygen and pressurization systems were all that stood between the life-crushing vacuum of space and the person riding inside. If the capsule wasn't strong enough to withstand the intense forces of the launch, it would explode. Every wire, every switch, every gauge, every component had to be tested and retested to make sure that it worked flawlessly.

Success depended on the engineers' mastery of the laws of physics and mathematics. The spacecraft demanded extreme precision and accuracy. Even a simple error would have catastrophic consequences. There seemed to be an infinite number of ways things could go wrong, and only one way to get it right.

America's Astronaut

Nobody understood the risks of space flight better than astronaut John Glenn. The former US Marine Corps test pilot had been chosen as the astronaut for America's first orbital flight. He pushed his body to the physical limit to prepare for the mission, and he worked tirelessly on the simulators and trainers, preparing for every failure scenario the engineers could imagine. He

John Glenn practices escaping from the Mercury capsule in the Back River, Hampton, Virginia. **NASA-Langley.**

knew that his life depended on his readiness.

As a test pilot, Glenn knew that the only way to remove all risk was to cancel the mission. He understood that he was likely to encounter some unforeseen problems, so he did his best to be ready for them. The preparations took longer than expected, and Project Mercury's launch was pushed back from late 1960 to July 1961 and then to 1962.

The Russians didn't slow down. In August 1961, they completed a seventeen-orbit flight, nearly a full day in space. The Soviet successes put even more pressure on NASA to get the mission off the ground.

In addition to the technical challenges, the launch team had to deal with the weather. Overcast skies at Cape Canaveral, Florida, delayed takeoff on two more dates. Finally, the date was set: February 20, 1962.

John Glenn handled the delays with patience and grace. He stayed in top condition and remained focused. Before taking off, he asked the engineers to complete one more check: he asked them to double-check the math that had been done by the electronic computers.

Many of the astronauts didn't fully trust the electronic number cruncher machines. As former test pilots, they staked their reputations — and their lives — on maintaining constant and direct control over their planes. A tiny error in judgment or a second of delay could mean disaster. The Mercury mission linked the spacecraft with the electronic computers on the ground. The astronauts worried: What if the computer lost power or seized up during the flight?

When the Space Task Group bought more

powerful computers, the trajectory equations were programmed into the machines, so that they could automatically guide and control the rocket and send information about the capsule's position back to Mission Control. If the rocket misfired and sent the capsule into an incorrect orbit, the computer would alert the flight controllers, who had the power to abort the mission. The capsule would detach from the rocket and land safely in the sea, where the astronaut could be rescued.

Once successfully launched, the capsule would push through the atmosphere and settle into orbit. It would separate from the rocket and establish new communications connections with the ground stations. The spacecraft would send data back to the tracking stations, which would capture the signals with their sixty-four-foot receiving dishes.

The Goddard Space Center in Maryland would also send Mission Control in Texas data about the spaceship's position. Hovering over the giant map of the world at Mission Control was a little cutout of a Mercury capsule, suspended on a wire. As data came into Mission Control, the image of the capsule would move across the map. While it was an unsophisticated map by today's standards, at the time, it helped the engineers follow the flight path.

The capsule's signal would bounce from one tracking station to another as it moved. The data would allow the controllers to ask: Where was the capsule compared to where they had calculated it to be at a given time? Was it too high, too low, too slow, too fast? They would constantly refine their data and make adjustments. This information would be used to determine exactly when the capsule's rockets should fire to bring the spacecraft back to Earth.

For the mission to succeed, the hardware, the software, and the human beings had to function properly. A breakdown in any component would be tragic, and it would all unfold on live television. The human computers crunching numbers were something the astronauts understood and trusted. The women mathematicians dominated their mechanical calculators the same way the test pilots dominated their planes. Spaceship-flying computers might be the future, but John Glenn didn't have to trust them. He did trust the human computer, Katherine Johnson.

"Get the girl to check the numbers," Glenn said.

If Katherine Johnson said the numbers

were good, he was ready to go.

Countdown

The space age and the television age were coming into their own at the same time. NASA understood that they were making history and that the events taking place should be broadcast to the world and recorded for history. The agency sent a film crew to each of the tracking stations, recording the communications teams as they completed their preflight checkouts. The footage showed the second-by-second drama in Mission Control as white men in white shirts and black ties faced long desks with communications consoles. Headphones on, serious expressions on their faces, the men stared up at an enormous electronic map of the world on the wall in front of them.

Because of her close working relationship with the pioneers of the Space Task Group, it was Katherine Johnson who found herself in a position to make the most immediate contribution to the Mercury mission.

When the phone call came in to Katherine Johnson's office at Langley, she was sitting at her desk. She overheard the call with the engineer who picked up. She knew she was "the girl" being discussed in the phone

Mercury Control at Cape Canaveral Air Force Station in Florida. US Navy Naval Aviation News, April 1962.

conversation. Astronaut John Glenn didn't know her name, but she was the one he was talking about when he wanted someone to double-check the numbers.

Katherine knew the numbers he meant: the ones that described the trajectories of an orbital mission around Earth, just like her first research report, the one she had worked on with the engineer Ted Skopinski. In the final section of the report, Katherine had calculated by hand two different sample orbits, plugging numbers into the equations in the report. Then she compared her results to the results from the IBM electronic computer, which had been programmed to calculate the same equations.

At the time, it turned out that there was "very good agreement" between the IBM's output and Katherine's calculations: Katherine and the machine got the same numbers. This work double-checking the electronic computer was a dress rehearsal for the work that was now required: checking the numbers not for a sample orbit, but for a real mission, with an astronaut on board.

Confidence

Though Katherine Johnson didn't usually panic in stressful situations, she was very nervous about the task in front of her. But she was confident in her math skills, so she organized herself at her desk. Thick stacks of data sheets and trajectory equations surrounded her work space. Instead of generating numbers and sending them to be checked by the computer, Katherine worked in reverse. She took the data from the computer and ran it through her own calculations. She wanted to see very good agreement between her numbers and those generated by the computer.

Katherine worked through every minute of a three-orbit mission. It took a day and a half of watching the numbers pile up until she had completed the task. When she delivered the data sheets to the Project

Mercury engineers, she had no doubt that her numbers were correct.

February 20, 1962

February 20, 1962, dawned bright and clear, and 135 million people tuned in to watch the launch unfold on live television. Katherine Johnson sat in the office, breathlessly watching the news coverage.

At 9:47 a.m. Eastern Standard Time, the Atlas rocket boosted *Friendship 7* into orbit. Ground control cleared John Glenn for seven orbits around Earth.

During the first orbit, the capsule's automatic control system began to act up, causing the capsule to pull back and forth, like a badly aligned car. Glenn smoothed it out by switching the system to manual and acting as if he were flying a plane.

At the end of the second orbit, a warning light indicated that the heat shield was loose. A heat shield is the outer covering on a spacecraft that protects it from extreme heat when the craft reenters Earth's atmosphere. Without that firewall, there was nothing standing between Glenn and the 3,000-degree temperatures — almost as hot as the surface of the sun — that would build up around the capsule as it passed back into Earth's atmosphere.

Mission Control had a solution: at the end of the third orbit, after the retro-rockets fired, Glenn was to keep the rocket pack attached to the spacecraft instead of getting rid of it as was standard procedure. The NASA engineers hoped that the rocket would keep the loose heat shield in place.

At four hours and thirty-three minutes into the flight, the rockets fired. John Glenn adjusted the capsule to the correct position — and waited.

The spaceship slowed down and pulled out of its orbit, heading down. At that point — the most dangerous part of the reentry — the signals flickered, then went silent.

There was no signal from *Friendship 7*.

The engineers tried to figure out what had gone wrong, but there was nothing Mission Control could do.

Silence.

One minute passed.

Then two.

Three.

Everyone feared the worst: that the heat shield had failed and the spacecraft had been burned.

The team struggled to reconnect with the spacecraft.

Ten minutes passed. Eleven. Twelve. Thirteen.

Fourteen minutes after the signal silenced, John Glenn's voice returned. He was alive!

The spaceship continued its descent, with the computer predicting a perfect landing. When *Friendship 7* splashed down it was off target by just forty miles, and that minor error was only because the estimated weight of the capsule during reentry included the added weight of the rocket that had remained in place.

The computers — both electronic and human — had worked flawlessly. Twenty-one minutes after landing, astronaut John Glenn was safely out of the water.

John Glenn was a hero. He had an audience with the president, a ticker tape parade in New York, and, from Maine to Moscow, large newspaper headlines cheering him. The African-American press cheered him. "All of us are happy to call him our Ace of Space," wrote an African-American columnist in the *Pittsburgh Courier.*

Nowhere was the hero's welcome as warm as in Hampton Roads, Virginia. Thirty thousand local residents turned out in mid-March to celebrate the man they considered their hometown hero. Glenn rode in the lead vehicle of a fifty-car parade that included the Mercury astronauts and their families. The twenty-two-mile route went through Hampton and Newport News.

The parade ended at a stadium where Glenn stood behind a podium with a sign reading "Spacetown, USA." The city of Hampton changed its official seal to depict a crab holding a Mercury capsule in its claw. It adopted the motto *E Praeteritis Futura* — Out of the Past, the Future.

John Glenn wasn't the only one being cheered. Word of Katherine Johnson's role in the mission made the rounds in the African-American community. On March 10, 1962, a photograph of Katherine Johnson was featured on the front page of the *Pittsburgh Courier.* The caption read: "Her name . . . in case you haven't already guessed it . . . is Katherine Johnson: mother, wife, career woman!" The article recounted Katherine's contributions to the work that sent Glenn's rocket through the sky.

Johnson attended the Hampton parade, allowing herself just a moment of pride at having been part of such an accomplishment. She didn't stay too long. She wanted to recognize the hard work and success of the team, but there was nothing more exhilarating for her than getting back to work on the next assignment.

22

AMERICA IS FOR EVERYBODY

"America is for everybody," said the US Department of Labor brochure issued in April 1963. The cover showed a young African-American boy, barefoot and dressed in a shirt and worn jeans, sitting on a dusty railroad track. In the text, President John F. Kennedy and Vice President Lyndon B. Johnson described the social and economic progress that African Americans had made since the end of slavery one hundred years before. One of the inspirational photographs inside the pamphlet showed Katherine Johnson working at her desk at Langley, already hard at work on the calculations that would one day help send an astronaut to the moon.

The same year that brochure was published, A. Philip Randolph — the civil rights leader who had pushed President Roosevelt to open war jobs to African Americans during World War II — planned the March on Washington for Jobs and Freedom, inviting political and religious leaders, and even well-known singers of many backgrounds, to participate. On August 28, 1963, an estimated three hundred thousand people marched through the nation's capital, gathering on the National Mall to hear a series of speeches. The defining moment of the event came when thirty-four-year-old Dr. Martin Luther King Jr. addressed the crowd. Shortly after he began speaking, Mahalia Jackson, one of the singers who had been invited to perform at the event, urged Dr. King to share his deepest feelings with the crowd. "Tell them about the dream, Martin!" she said to him, urging him to speak to the crowd from his heart.

King knew she was right. He set aside his prepared remarks and put both hands on the lectern. He then gave his country — and the world — seventeen of the most memorable minutes in history. Dr. King's "I Have a Dream" speech reminded all the citizens of the nation that the African-American dream and the American dream were one and the same.

Dr. Martin Luther King Jr. addresses a crowd from the steps of the Lincoln Memorial as he delivers his "I Have a Dream" speech during the March on Washington on August 28, 1963. United States Marine Corps.

The Dream at Langley

In many ways, Dorothy Vaughan was living the American dream. The director of the Langley Research Center sent Dorothy a letter acknowledging her twenty years of service to the federal government. He presented her with a gold-and-ruby lapel pin during the center's annual awards ceremony. By the standards of their families and many associates, Dorothy and the other

African-American employees at NASA had secured professional jobs and the respect of their colleagues. They were part of the visions that Martin Luther King Jr. and Presidents Kennedy and Johnson had for a more tolerant and just America.

But there was still progress to be made, even at Langley. Of all the black employees working in research at Langley in the early 1960s, there were only five categorized as engineers and sixteen with the title mathematician, including Dorothy. Langley's director wrote to NASA headquarters in Washington, DC, lamenting that "very few Negroes" were applying for open science and engineering positions at the laboratory.

"There is no doubt that one of the reasons they do not apply is that they do not believe that the living conditions in the area would be favorable to them because the Langley Research Center, which is completely integrated, is situated in a community where social segregation based on color is still practiced to a certain extent," he wrote.

Langley redoubled its recruiting efforts. In the mid-1960s, with dreams of working at NASA, greater numbers of African-American college students found their way to the research center.

The Next Generation

When she wasn't at work, Katherine Johnson spent a great deal of her free time at community service activities and at church. After church one Sunday in 1967, Katherine saw a new face in the crowd. She went over and introduced herself to the young woman, who was there with her husband and two daughters.

"I'm Katherine Johnson," she said.

"Yes, I know," said Christine Mann Darden. "You're Joylette's mother." Katherine's daughter Joylette had met Christine in college, at Hampton Institute. Katherine and Christine had met once before, at a sorority function, though they hadn't seen one another in years.

Since graduating from Hampton Institute, Christine had started working as a math teacher, and had gotten married. Earlier that spring, she had completed her master's degree program at Virginia State University, a black college, and she had visited the school placement office during her final semester of study. "We wish you'd been here yesterday," said the placement officer. "NASA was here interviewing."

The woman handed Christine an application for federal employment. Christine applied, and NASA offered her a position as a

Christine Darden working at the wind tunnel control at the Langley Research Center in 1974. **NASA-Langley.**

data analyst. Once in Hampton Roads, she saw Katherine Johnson and other former West Computers on a regular basis both at work and in the community. Christine had gone to school with Katherine's daughters, and she already felt a connection to her. Christine was part of the next generation of women at NASA, those who would rely on the pioneers like Katherine and Dorothy and Mary for inspiration and guidance.

Katherine Johnson invited Christine to join the choir at church. The two women got to know one another outside of the of-

Christine Darden poses in a wind tunnel with a model of a supersonic aircraft at Langley Research Center in the early 1970s. NASA-Langley.

fice, but they never worked together. Because Katherine was so modest, it would be years before Christine knew the full scope of her work. When someone acknowledged her achievements, Katherine said, "Well, I'm just doing my job."

For Katherine, doing her job meant quietly sharing the joy when missions went well, as well as grieving with the others when missions failed. Like the others at NASA, Katherine was devastated in January 1967 when an electrical fire on board the *Apollo 1* command module took the lives of three astronauts: Ed White, Roger Chaffee, and Gus Grissom.

The tragic end of *Apollo 1* shook NASA to its core. The astronauts had been on the ground inside the module, on the launch pad in Cape Canaveral, when an electrical spark caused a fire that flashed through the inside of the craft, killing all three men inside. The engineers redesigned the spacecraft, carefully discovering then fixing the flaws that had caused the fire. They honored the dead by learning from the mistakes of the past and carrying on with future missions.

Each experience offered important information that could be applied to future flights. In the 1960s, the Apollo program built on its successes, steadily aiming toward a landmark achievement of the space program: a manned mission to the moon.

Mission to the Moon

The 238,900-mile mission to the moon would take six days: three days to get there and three days to come back. The ambitious plan included twenty-one hours exploring the surface of the moon for two astronauts in the lunar lander, a separate vehicle that would drive across the moon while the service module circled above.

The plan sounded simple, but Katherine Johnson knew better than anyone that if any aspect of the *Apollo 11* mission to the moon went wrong, the astronauts could be stranded in space, never again to see their earthly home. Years later, Katherine would say that working on the math that co-ordinated the orbiting Apollo Command and Service Module (CSM) — one part of the spaceship that would remain "parked" in orbit around the Moon — with the ship's lunar lander — the rowboat of a module that would take the astronauts from the CSM down to the moon's surface — was the highlight of her career at NASA.

The leadership of the Space Task Group set a risk standard of "three nines" for the space missions. In other words, it required that every aspect of the program — every part, every plan, every person — succeed 999 times out of 1,000. The astronauts were prepared to give their lives to their mission, but they didn't want to die because of a math error.

Katherine Johnson worked long hours to make sure the astronauts stayed safe. She arrived at the office early, went home in the late afternoon to check on her girls, and sometimes came back to work in the eve-

ning, maintaining a schedule of fourteen-
or sixteen-hour days.

She and the engineers she worked with
asked each other what-if questions: What if
the computers went out? What if there was
an electrical failure on board the spacecraft?
What if something went wrong? They had
to think ahead, anticipating and solving
every problem they could think of before it
happened.

23

ONE SMALL STEP

A human being on the moon! It was hard for most people to believe that something that humankind had dreamed of for thousands of years was finally coming true. It also amazed many Americans to learn what an expensive trip it was. Together, the Apollo missions cost a mind-boggling $24 billion, or about $156 billion in today's dollars.

Not everyone believed that the exploration of space was worth the astronomical price tag. A few days before the *Apollo 11* launch, two hundred protesters marched outside Cape Canaveral as part of the Poor People's Campaign, a movement designed to bring attention to the problems facing poor people of all colors. At the beginning of the 1960s, the space program and the civil rights movement shared a sense of optimism. Scientific idealists believed that technical know-how would make the future better, and civil rights advocates fought hard to ensure that everyone, regardless of race or color or background, would receive the blessings of democracy that the United States Constitution promised all of the country's citizens. By the end of the decade, some of those civil rights leaders argued that the billions of dollars spent to send a handful of people to the moon could help many millions of poor people right here on Earth. Activists challenged NASA to consider the worthiness of the space program when disadvantaged people on Earth could barely put food on the table.

Many people also asked why there weren't any black astronauts and why there were only a few black engineers or scientists working for NASA. African Americans believed that outer space belonged to people of every race and the space program should, too. Not many of them knew that in Hampton, Virginia, black women like Katherine and Dorothy and Mary and Christine were working hard, using their mathematical talents to help the United States.

Landing

On July 20, 1969, more than six hundred million people around the world sat in front of their TVs, eager for their first close-up look at the heavenly body that they had only ever seen in the sky from their earthly home. While the astronauts continued their 238,900-mile journey to the moon, Katherine Johnson had just finished a much shorter trip. She and about one hundred of her sorority sisters had come to a quiet hotel in the Pennsylvania mountains for a weekend retreat. Even there, however, everyone was eager for news of the historic voyage. The other women crowded around the hotel's small black-and-white television, listening to the news anchors and watching the screen as the astronauts glided closer and closer to their destination. The moon mission was so complex that it had taken more than four hundred thousand people, working as a team, to send the spacecraft safely on its way. Since the early 1960s, when President Kennedy announced that he wanted America to land a person on the moon, Katherine Johnson had worked hard on the analysis that had eventually made this day possible. She had given years of hard work to NASA and its mission. But the hardest part might have been to sit watching the astronauts moving away from Earth through the cold vacuum of space, bound for the moon. She knew there was no way she would be able to relax until the astronauts had landed on the moon, and returned safely back to Earth. Even with twenty-six manned flights under NASA's belt, this was different, and everyone knew it.

Katherine Johnson watched the television. The *Eagle*, the lunar lander, a crablike mechanical contraption carrying astronauts Neil Armstrong and Buzz Aldrin, emerged from the *Apollo* command module and descended to the surface of the moon. At 10:38 p.m. Eastern Daylight Time on July 20, 1969, humankind set foot for the first time in history on a heavenly body other than Earth: astronaut Neil Armstrong climbed down a ladder and stepped onto the moon.

"That's one small step for a man," he said, "one giant leap for mankind."

The actual landing had been one part of the mission that had been impossible to rehearse — and the most dangerous. The *Apollo 11* astronauts had given the mission only a so-so chance of success. Neil Armstrong thought they had a 50-50 chance of landing on the moon on the first try.

Katherine Johnson had confidence: she knew her numbers were right. She always expected the best. "You have to expect progress to be made," she said.

Timing was everything. After the moon walk, Katherine knew the astronauts had a brief window to get back into the lunar lander and reconnect with the mother ship above. Then they had three long days on the highway back to Earth, followed by a journey through the fire of the atmosphere and down to the ocean below. She knew she would hold her breath until the space pioneers had been lifted from the ocean by the waiting navy ships.

But the mission was a success, from beginning to end, takeoff to splashdown.

The astronauts had returned to their home on Earth safely. Katherine enjoyed a bit of ease, but only for a moment. NASA still had six more Apollo missions planned, and there was always the thrill of the next discovery.

Now that NASA had successfully landed astronauts on the moon, Katherine and some of her coworkers had talked about a mission to Mars. Others dreamed about going even farther away from Earth, embarking on a grand tour that would send a spacecraft hopping from Mars to Jupiter to

Saturn, like a stone skipped across a glassy lake.

It wouldn't be easy, but the nimble minds at Langley could make it a reality, Katherine thought. Why should flying a person to Mars be any less achievable than sending a man into orbit around Earth or landing a man on the moon? One thing built on the next. Katherine Johnson knew: once you took the first step, anything was possible.

TIMELINE OF IMPORTANT
HISTORICAL EVENTS

1861–1865 Civil War

January 1, 1863 Emancipation Proclamation

1890–1965 Jim Crow Laws

1903 Wright Brothers make the first powered flight

1915 Federal Government establishes the National Advisory Committee for Aeronautics (NACA)

October 29, 1929 Black Tuesday, the start of the Great Depression

1929–1939 The Great Depression

1935 The Langley Memorial Aeronautical Laboratory establishes the first female computing pool

1939–1945 World War II

1940–1952 Tuskegee Airmen, a group of African-American military pilots, many of whom served in World War II

June 25, 1941 The Fair Employment Practice Committee is established

May 1943 The Langley Memorial Laboratory establishes the first segregated computing pool for black women

June 6, 1944 D-Day: The Allied invasion of Normandy, France, during World War II. It was the largest seaborne invasion in history.

August 14–15, 1945 V-J Day: Victory over Japan Day

September 2, 1945 The signing of the surrender document, officially ending World War II

June 3, 1946 The decision for *Morgan v. Virginia,* the legal case making segregation on interstate buses illegal

1947–1991 Cold War

April 5, 1951 Julius and Ethel Rosenberg's sentencing for espionage

1954–1968 Civil Rights Movement

May 17, 1954 *Brown v. Board of Education* ruling declares separate schools for black and white students was unconstitutional

December 1, 1955 Rosa Parks refuses to give up her seat in the front of a public bus

October 4, 1957 The Soviet Union launches *Sputnik* and the dawn of the Space Age begins

1958 The Space Act of 1958 creates the National Aeronautics and Space Administration (NASA)

1958 Launch of Project Mercury. Project Mercury was officially approved on October 7, 1958, and lasted until 1963.

1960 Greensboro sit-ins: a series of nonviolent protests in Greensboro, North Carolina

January 31, 1961 Ham, the first chimp to be launched into space

April 12, 1961 Russian cosmonaut Yuri Gagarin is the first human in space and the first human to orbit Earth.

May 5, 1961 Project Mercury's first manned mission, with astronaut Alan Shepard, is a success

February 20, 1962 John Glenn flies the *Friendship 7* mission and becomes the first American to orbit Earth

August 28, 1963 Martin Luther King gives his "I Have a Dream" speech

July 20, 1969 *Apollo 11* astronauts Neil Armstrong and Edwin "Buzz" Aldrin become the first humans to land on the Moon

GLOSSARY

Aeronautics: The science of flying.

Atmosphere: The gasses surrounding Earth or other planets.

Gravity: The force that attracts a body toward the center of Earth or another large mass.

Hypersonic: A speed exceeding Mach 5, or five times the speed of sound.

Mach 1: The speed of sound at sea level with an air temperature of 59 degrees Fahrenheit, or about 761.2 miles per hour. The speed varies slightly at different temperatures because gas molecules move more slowly at colder temperatures.

National Advisory Committee for Aeronautics (NACA): The United States agency started in 1915 to supervise and direct the scientific study of the problems of flight; in 1958, NACA ended and NASA was formed.

National Aeronautics and Space Adminis-

tration (NASA): The independent government agency responsible for the civilian (as opposed to military) space program; NASA was founded in 1958.

Orbit: The curved path of an object or spacecraft as it revolves around a star, planet, or moon.

Project Mercury: The first human space flight program in the United States; it ran from 1958 to 1963, with the goal of putting a man in orbit around Earth.

Rocket: A high-speed streamlined vehicle propelled by burning fuel.

Satellite: A man-made object placed in orbit around Earth, its moon, or another planet to collect information or assist with communication.

Sonic boom: The sound associated with shock waves created by an object moving faster than the speed of sound; examples include a bullet blast or the cracking of a bullwhip.

Space race: The competition between nations — especially the United States and the Soviet Union — regarding space exploration.

Speed of sound: The distance traveled by a sound wave in a fixed period of time; sound travels most slowly in gasses, faster in water, and fastest in solids.

Sputnik: A series of satellites launched by the Soviet Union. *Sputnik 1,* launched on October 4, 1957, was the first satellite to orbit Earth.

Supersonic: Speed that is faster than the speed of sound.

Theoretical engineer: An engineer using mathematics to solve problems, without testing in real-world simulations.

Trajectory: The path of an object as it moves through space.

Turbulence: The unsteady or irregular movement of air or water.

Variable: A factor or value that is likely to change; in a mathematical equation, the variable is the symbol representing the number we don't know yet.

Wind tunnel: A tool used in aeronautics research to study the effect of air moving over an object; tests done in wind tunnels attempt to simulate how an object would perform in flight so that researchers can improve on aircraft design.

SOURCE NOTES

Chapter 2: A Door Opens

"Reduce your household duties!" February 3, 1942, Langley Archives Collection, September 12, 2001.

"Victory through air power!" "What's My Name?" *Air Scoop,* June 14, 1946.

Chapter 3: Mobilization

"Paving the Way for Women Engineers": "Paving the Way for Women Engineers," *Norfolk Journal and Guide,* May 8, 1943.

"How soon could you be ready to start work?" Dorothy Vaughan, personnel file.

Chapter 4: A New Beginning

"What Can We Do to Win the War?" "Farmville," *Norfolk Journal and Guide,* November 28, 1942.

"You are hereby appointed Mathematician": Dorothy Vaughan, personnel file.

"Mrs. D. J. Vaughan, instructor in mathematics": Eloise Barker, "Farmville," *Norfolk Journal and Guide,* December 11, 1943.

"I'll be back for Christmas": Ann Vaughan Hammond, personal interview, June 30, 2014.

Chapter 5: The Double V

"Four Freedoms": Franklin D. Roosevelt, "The Four Freedoms: Message to the Seventy-Seventh Congress," January 6, 1941.

"Help us to get some of the blessings of democracy": P. B. Young, "Service or Betrayal?" *Norfolk Journal and Guide,* April 25, 1942.

"Being an American of dark complexion": James G. Thompson, "Should I Sacrifice to Live Half-American?" *Pittsburgh Courier,* January 31, 1942.

"Let colored Americans adopt the double VV": Ibid.

Chapter 6: The "Colored" Computers

"land of desolation, a land of marshes and mosquitoes": "The First Epistle of the NACAites," *Air Scoop,* January 19, 1945.

"single best and biggest aeronautical research complex in the world": James R. Hansen, *Engineer in Charge: A History of the Langley Aeronautical Laboratory, 1917–1958* (Washington, DC: National Aeronautics and Space Administration, 1987), 188.

"They are going to fire you over that sign, Miriam": Miriam Mann Harris, personal interview, May 6, 2014.

Chapter 7: War Birds

"It's best described as a 'pilot's airplane' ": "New US 'Mustang' Heralded as Best Fighter Plane of 1943," *Washington Post,* November 27, 1942.

"It will get you up in the air, let you do your job": "Tuskegee Airman Reunited with 'Best Plane in the World,' " National Aeronautics and Space Administration, June 10, 2004.

"You tell it to someone who repeats it to someone": *Air Scoop,* March 25–31, 1944.

"brain busters," "NACA nuts," "weirdos":

Parker Rouse, "Early Days at Langley Were Colorful," *Daily Press,* March 25, 1990.

"Woe unto thee if they shall make thee a computer": "Second Epistle of the NACA-ites," *Air Scoop,* January 26, 1945.

Chapter 8: The Duration

"You're not going to take my babies": Hammond interview, June 20, 2014.

"decrease for women workers, both white and colored": "Hampton Roads Area Faces Drastic Cut in Employment," *Washington Post,* October 21, 1945.

"Many husbands will return home to find": "Jobs Open for Whites Only," *Norfolk Journal and Guide,* September 1, 1945.

"the most dangerous idea ever seriously considered": Harry Byrd, quoted in Glenn Feldman, *The Great Melding: War, the Dixiecrat Rebellion, and the Southern Model for America's New Conservatism* (Tuscaloosa: University of Alabama Press, 2015), 211.

"war-devastated populations in Europe": "Realtors Win Efforts for Post-war Riddance of Federal Housing Units," *Norfolk Journal and Guide,* June 30, 1945.

"not temporary in character": Ibid.

Chapter 9: Breaking Barriers

"Effective this date, Dorothy V. Vaughan": Eldridge H. Derring "To All Concerned: Appointment of Head of West Area Computers Unit," January 8, 1951. National Archives and Records Administration, Philadelphia.

Chapter 10: No Limits

"Hold on a minute!" Katherine Johnson, personal interview, April 3, 2014.

"too fast to be identified": Stephen Joiner, "The Jet That Shocked the West," *Air and Space Magazine,* December 2013.

"Russia Said to Have Fastest Fighter Plane": Leon Schloss, *Norfolk Journal and Guide,* February 18 1950.

"the Russians expended at least three times the man power": Ibid.

"For America to continue its present challenged supremacy": Ibid.

"The laboratory has one work unit composed entirely of Negro women": W. Kemble Johnson to NACA, "Fair Employment." November 21, 1951.

Chapter 11: The Area Rule

"Can you direct me to the bathroom?" Richard Stradling, "Retired Engineer Remembers Segregated Langley," *Daily Press,* February 8, 1998.
"Why don't you come work for me?" Ibid.

Chapter 12: An Exceptional Mind

"You would make a good research mathematician": Katherine Johnson, March 11, 2011.
"unusually capable": Albert P. Kalme, "Racial Desegregation and Integration in American Education: The Case History of West Virginia State College, 1891–1973" (PhD dissertation, University of Ottawa, 1976), 149.

Chapter 13: Turbulence

"Either give her a raise or send her back to me": Johnson interview, September 17, 1992.
"one of the most interesting things [she] had ever read," Katherine Johnson, National Visionary video.
"I want to move our girls out of the proj-

ects," Katherine Goble Moore, July 31, 2014.

"It is very important that you don't show the girls": Ibid.

"You will have my clothes ironed and ready": Ibid.

Chapter 14: Progress

"electronic calculator": "Announce New Research Device," *Air Scoop,* March 28, 1947.

"Integration is going to come": Ann Vaughan Hammond, untitled biographical sketch of Dorothy Vaughan, undated, in author's possession.

"Effects on Nose Angle and Mach Number": Langley Aeronautical Laboratory, September 1958.

"You will never do that again to this man": Thomas Byrdsong, personal interview, October 4, 2014.

Chapter 15: Young, Gifted, and Black

"Red-Made Satellite Flashes Across US": *Daily Press,* October 5, 1957.

"Sphere Tracked in 4 Crossings Over US": *New York Times,* October 5, 1957.

"small ball in the air": David S. F. Potree,

"One Small Ball in the Air: October 4, 1957–November 3, 1957," *NASA's Origins and the Dawn of the Space Age, Monographs in Aerospace History,* National Aerospace and Space Administration, September 1998.

"Who can say that it was not the institution of the Jim Crow": Christine Darden, personal interview, May 3, 2012.

"I just came to let you all know that the Supreme Court": Christine Darden, "Growing Up in the South During *Brown v. Board,*" *Unbound* magazine, March 5, 2015.

"education, honesty, hard work, and character": Wini Warren, *Black Women Scientists in the United States* (Bloomington: Indiana University Press, 2000), 75.

Chapter 16: What a Difference a Day Makes

"First in space means first, period": Lyndon B. Johnson, quoted in Walter A. McDougall, *The Heavens and Earth: A Political History of the Space Age* (Baltimore: Johns Hopkins University Press, 1997).

"provide for the widest practicable and appropriate dissemination": National Aero-

nautics and Space Act of 1958, www.hq
.nasa.gov/office/pao/History/spaceact
.html.

Chapter 17: Writing the Textbook on Space

"Present your case, build it": Claiborne R.
Hicks, interview with Kevin M. Rasnak,
April 11, 2000.

"Why can't I go to the editorial meetings?"
Katherine Johnson, September 27, 2013.

"they were all the same," Katherine Johnson, personal interview, December 27,
2010.

"Let her go," Katherine Johnson, September
27, 2013.

Chapter 18: With All Deliberate Speed

"Let me do it": Katherine Johnson, History
Makers Video.

"Katherine should finish the report": Wini
Warren, *Black Women Scientists in the
United States* (Bloomington: Indiana
University Press, 2000), 143.

"Determination of Azimuth Angle at Burnout": Ted Skopinski and Katherine Johnson, Langley Research Center, 1960.

Chapter 19: Model Behavior

"The car and driver together": Soap Box Derby Rules, 1960.

"I want to be an engineer like my mother": "Hampton Youth Captures Area Derby Championship," *Norfolk Journal and Guide,* July 2, 1960.

Chapter 20: Degrees of Freedom

"We want to be treated as American citizens": Jimmy Knight, "Hamptonian's View: Jail Will Not Stop Student Protest," *Norfolk Journal and Guide,* March 5, 1960.

"We could have beaten them": Christopher Kraft, *Flight: My Life in Mission Control* (New York: Dutton, 2001), 132.

"I believe that this nation should commit itself": John F. Kennedy, "Urgent National Needs: A Special Message to Congress by President Kennedy," May 25, 1961.

Chapter 21: Out of the Past, the Future

"Get the girl to check the numbers": John Glen, quoted in Swendon, Grimwood, and Alexander, *This New Ocean,* 273–283.

"her name . . . in case you haven't already guessed it": "Lady Mathematician Plays a

Key Role in Glenn Space Flight," *Pittsburgh Courier,* March 10, 1962.

Chapter 22: America Is for Everybody

"America is for everybody": US Department of Labor, April 1963.
"There is no doubt that one of the reasons": Floyd L. Thompson to James E. Webb, December 29, 1961, National Archives and Records Administration, Philadelphia.

Chapter 23: One Small Step

"You have to expect progress to be made": Katherine Johnson, personal interview, December 27, 2010.

FURTHER READING

Abdul-Jabbar, Kareem and Raymond Obstfeld, and Ben Boos and A. G. Ford (illustrators). *What Color Is My World?: The Lost History of African-American Inventors.* Somerville, MA: Candlewick, 2012.

Borden, Louise and Mary Kay Kroeger, and Teresa Flavin (illustrator). *Fly High!: The Story of Bessie Coleman.* New York: Aladdin, 2004.

Gibson, Karen Bush. *Women in Space: 23 Stories of First Flights, Scientific Missions, and Gravity-Breaking Adventures (Women of Action).* Chicago, Illinois: Chicago Review Press, 2014.

Ignotofsky, Rachel. *Women in Science: 50 Fearless Pioneers Who Changed the World.* New York: Ten Speed Press, 2016.

Schatz, Kate, and Miriam Klein Stahl (illustrator). *Rad American Women A-Z: Rebels, Trailblazers, and Visionaries who*

Shaped Our History . . . and Our Future! San Francisco, CA: City Lights Publishers, 2015.

Stone, Tanya Lee. *Almost Astronauts: 13 Women Who Dared to Dream.* Somerville, MA: Candlewick, 2009.

Swaby, Rachel. *Trailblazers: 33 Women in Science Who Changed the World.* New York: Delacorte Books for Young Readers, 2016.

Thimmesh, Catherine, and Melissa Sweet (illustrator). *Girls Think of Everything: Stories of Ingenious Inventions by Women.* New York: HMH Books for Young Readers, 2002.

Warren, Wini. *Black Women Scientists in the United States.* Bloomington: Indiana University Press, 2000.

INDEX

ABOUT THE AUTHOR

Margot Lee Shetterly was born in Hampton, Virginia, in 1969. She is a graduate of the University of Virginia's McIntire School of Commerce. After college she worked in investment banking for several years. Her other career moves have included working in the media industry for the website Volume.com, publishing an English language magazine, *Inside Mexico*; marketing consultant in the Mexican tourism industry; and writing. *Hidden Figures* is her first book, a *New York Times* Bestseller and was optioned for a feature film.